THE BEST OF P[...]

PARIS WALKS

Step off the plane and head right for the newest, hippest café in town. Find out where to get the best fish in the city or where they have locally brewed beer on tap. In *Moon Paris Walks*, our authors give you inside information on numerous hidden gems. Skip the busy shopping streets and stroll through the city at your own pace, taking in a local attraction on your way to the latest and greatest concept stores. Savor every second and make your trip a truly great experience.

PARIS-BOUND!

You're about to discover Paris—the city of wide avenues, world-famous monuments, and of course, *la vie Parisienne*. Start the day with a cup of coffee and a croissant, which—just like the locals—you can have in a café standing at the counter. Shop in amazing stores, from those of top designers to small, vintage boutiques in one of the city's many charming neighborhoods. Don't forget to take in some culture with a visit to a museum or a walk in one of the many parks and gardens. Plus, there is good food and good wine to be had in every neighborhood. We'll show you where.

ABOUT THIS BOOK

In this book, local authors share with you the genuine highlights of their city. Discover the city by foot and at your own pace, so you can relax and experience the local lifestyle without having to do a lot of preparation beforehand. That means more time for you—what we call "time to momo." Our walks take you past our favorite restaurants, cafés, museums, galleries, shops, and other notable attractions—places we ourselves like to go to.

None of the places mentioned here have paid to appear in either the text or the photos, and all text has been written by an independent editorial staff. This is true for the places in this book as well as for the information in the **time to momo app** and all the latest tips, themed routes, neighborhood information, blogs and the selection of best hotels on **www.timetomomo.com**.

LOCAL
IRENE KLEIN

CITY
PARIS

WORK & OTHER ACTIVITIES
TOUR GUIDE

Paris—the most beautiful city on Earth! That is, according to Irene, who's been here since 2007. She works as a tour guide and takes visitors around Paris and the rest of France. For Irene, working in museums and monuments is pure luxury. She lives in the hip 11th *arrondissement*, and in her free time, loves to picnic in the park and drink wine in nice cafés.

PRACTICAL INFORMATION

The six walks in this book allow you to discover the best neighborhoods in the city by foot and at your own pace. The routes will take you past museums and notable attractions, but more importantly, they'll show you where to go for good food, drinks, shopping, entertainment, and an overall good time. Check out the map at the front of this book to see which areas the walks will take you through.

Each route is clearly indicated on a detailed map at the beginning of each chapter. The map also specifies where each place is located. The color of the number tells you what type of venue it is (see the key at the bottom of this page). A description of each place is then given later in the chapter.

Without taking into consideration extended stops at various locations, each route will take a maximum of three hours. The approximate distance is indicated at the top of the page, before the directions.

PRICE INDICATION
Along with the address and contact details for each location, we give an idea of how much you can expect to spend there. Unless otherwise stated, the amount given in restaurant listings is the average price of a main course. For sights and attractions, we indicate the cost of a regular full-price ticket.

GOOD TO KNOW
Paris consists of the area between the two ring roads that encircle the city: the Boulevard Extérieur and the Périphérique. Everything outside of these roads is considered the *banlieues*. The River Seine runs through the city, splitting it into

```
┌─────────────────────────────────────────────────┐
│                    LEGEND                         │
├─────────────────────────────────────────────────┤
│                                                   │
│  ● >> SIGHTS & ATTRACTIONS    ● >> FOOD & DRINK   │
│  ● >> SHOPPING                ● >> MORE TO EXPLORE │
│                                                   │
└─────────────────────────────────────────────────┘
```

the Rive Droite (Right Bank) and the Rive Gauche (Left Bank). In addition, Paris is divided into 20 *arrondissements* (districts). Each arrondissement has a name and a number. The first, called *Louvre*, is located in the very center of the city. From there, the arrondissements spiral outwards clockwise through the city. The number of the arrondissement is generally indicated on the street signs.

Most stores in Paris open around 10:00am and close around 7:30pm, although small shops and some grocery stores close between noon and 3:00pm. Small neighborhood convenience stores are an exception and usually don't close until midnight. Many grocery stores and food markets are open Sunday mornings but closed on Mondays. In the traditionally Jewish Marais neighborhood and in Montmartre, most shops are open on Sundays.

Stores in France have clearance sales twice a year: three weeks in July-August and three weeks in January. During these sales you can find some really good deals. Check the exact dates ahead of time because you don't want to miss this.

In August, many restaurants, cafés, and shops (such as bakeries and butchers) are closed the entire month for vacation. Be sure to keep this in mind.

MUSEUMS

With its beautiful, prestigious museums, Paris is paradise for museum lovers. But when it comes to opening hours, beware—some museums are closed Mondays, others Tuesdays. There is generally no rhyme or reason to it. The Paris Museum Pass *(www.parismuseumpass.com)* offers access to more than 60 museums and monuments. A two-day pass costs €42, a four-day pass €56, and a six-day pass €69, although you often have to pay extra for temporary exhibits beyond the permanent collection. You can purchase these passes at participating museums and monuments, or at the tourist office at 25 Rue des Pyramides. If you'd rather not wait in line, consider buying your tickets online beforehand. Often there is a separate entrance for people with pre-purchased tickets and the Museum Pass. Note that many museums offer free entrance to people from within the EU under the age of 26 and discounts to the disabled and seniors over 60. On the first Sunday of the month, some museums are also open to the general public free of charge.

FRENCH FOOD CULTURE

In France, people take food seriously. The French love to eat and to talk about food. The two most important meals are *le déjeuner* (lunch) and *le dîner* (dinner). *Le petit déjeuner* (breakfast), on the other hand, tends to be a relatively simple affair: coffee, tea or hot chocolate and a *tartine* (bread with jam) or croissant. Breakfast is eaten at home or in a café, most of which open early. In the morning, people in cafés take their coffee and croissant at the counter. This is perhaps not as comfortable as getting a table, but it's definitely cheaper—it can sometimes even be half the price. Order a *café* (espresso), *café allongé* (espresso diluted with hot water), *café crème* (espresso with warm milk), *café au lait* (espresso with cold milk) or a *noisette* (a small cup of espresso with a splash of cold milk). Lunch is usually eaten out. Many companies give their employees meal vouchers, called *ticket restaurant,* and lunch is often used to discuss business. Between 12:30pm and 2:30pm restaurants are therefore generally quite busy. A traditional French lunch consists of three courses, although you can opt for just an *entrée* (starter) or *plat* (main course). Don't forget to see if there is a *menu du jour* or *plat du jour* (daily specials). An increasingly popular dessert in Paris is the *café/thé gourmand:* Coffee or tea served alongside a dessert sampler. Parisians often work late in the evenings and generally don't eat until 8:00pm during the week, so restaurants don't open for dinner until around 7:30pm. On weekends restaurants don't start getting busy until after 9:00pm. Parisians love to eat out, so restaurants are usually packed. If you want to be sure to get a table, reserve ahead of time. After a meal, tipping isn't necessary. If you do leave a tip, it means you were especially satisfied, and of course this is appreciated. Never seat yourself in a restaurant—always let the server bring you to a table.

You may find that Parisians come across as being a little stuffy, but a friendly *"Bonjour"* whenever you enter a restaurant or shop can work wonders. Make sure it's always the first thing you say wherever you go and you'll be surprised at the service you get.

PUBLIC HOLIDAYS

In addition to days like Easter, Pentecost, and Ascension Day, which don't fall on a specific date, the following are official holidays in France:

January 1 > New Year's Day
May 1 > Labor Day
May 8 > Victory in Europe Day (end of WWII in 1945)
July 14 > Bastille Day (Quatorze Juillet)
August 15 > Assumption Day
November 1 > All Saints' Day
November 11 > Armistice Day (end of WWI in 1918)
December 25 > Christmas Day

On June 21, the evening of the summer solstice, Paris celebrates the Fête de la Musique. It is a day of musical revelry when people everywhere—in the streets, cafés, bars, concert halls, or at home—listen to and make music and dance in the streets.

From the evening of July 13 until early in the morning of Quatorze Juillet you can dance in fire halls at the Bal des Pompiers—Fireman's Ball. Various festivities are organized throughout the city on July 14.

Starting in early January, cakes known as *galettes des rois*—each with a little charm baked inside—begin to appear in French bakeries. Every French family buys these cakes. According to tradition, once the cake is cut the youngest person at the table gets to decide who gets which piece. Whoever finds the charm then has to buy the next cake.

HAVE ANY TIPS?
Shops and restaurants in Paris come and go fairly regularly. We do our best to keep the routes and contact details as up-to-date as possible, and this is

---

TUNED IN TO PARIS!

GO TO WWW.TIMETOMOMO.COM FOR THE LATEST TIPS
NEW ADDRESSES + UP-AND-COMING NEIGHBORHOODS
+ POP-UP STORES + CONCERTS + FESTIVALS + MUCH MORE

immediately reflected in our digital products. We also do our best to update the print edition as often as we can. However, if despite our best efforts there is a place that you can't find or if you have any other comments or tips about this book, please let us know. Email info@momedia.nl, or leave a message on **www.timetomomo.com**.

TRANSPORTATION

Paris is not only the City of Light, it is also the city of **cars.** In an effort to reduce traffic, Paris developed a reliable public transportation network that includes a subway system (Métro), commuter trains (RER), and buses. The same ticket can be used for all of these types of transportation. Tickets can be purchased at the ticket window or from machines in Métro stations, RER stations, and RATP bus stations, which are part of Paris's public transportation system. Individual tickets cost €1.80, but a bundle of ten—known as a *carnet*—is cheaper: €14.10.

The **Métro** runs every day between 5:30am and about 1:00am, or 2:00am on Saturdays—exact times vary per station. On Sundays, the Métro runs less frequently. Tickets are valid for one ride and transfers are allowed, provided you don't leave the station. The **RER** is a regional commuter train that extends into the suburbs but can also be used within Paris. RER lines don't stop as frequently as the Métro. The RER runs from 4:45am to 1:00am. Paris's many **buses** are also convenient for getting to know the city. You can find a map of Métro and RER lines at the back of this book. Paris's public transportation company, RATP, has a useful free app called Next Stop Paris (Visiter Paris en Métro).

As far as **taxi** prices go, Paris is pretty reasonable. It's also fairly easy to hail one of the 15,000 cabs that drive around the city. Note, however, that a taxi will only stop if it is at least 50 meters away from a designated taxi stand. When both the light and the big taxi sign on the roof are illuminated, the taxi is available, but if the sign is not on, the taxi is occupied. You can also arrange a cab by phone: Taxis G7 (phone: 01 41 27 66 99) and Taxis Bleus (phone: 08 91 70 10 10).

BIKING

Paris is becoming increasingly more **bike-friendly.** The city currently has some 400 kilometers of *pistes cyclables* (bike lanes). Every Sunday certain roads, such as those near the Canal St.-Martin, are closed to cars. However, the average Parisian driver is still not accustomed to sharing the road with cyclists, so always be alert. Keep in mind that sometimes bike lanes end suddenly or cross over sidewalks, and pedestrians don't always recognize the sound of a bike bell. So remember the word *"attention"* and be ready to use it to let people know you're coming.

Vélib', the city's **bike-share** program, has over 20,000 bikes spread across 1,800 stations *(www.velib.paris.fr)*. You'll see the docked gray bikes and information kiosks all around town. The system is simple: Use your credit card at any station's kiosk to buy a day pass (€1.70) or week pass (€8.00), then borrow any bike from a dock with a green light. You pay based on how long your bike is out of the dock. You can put your bike back in any available dock, but be sure that the green light goes back on when you do, otherwise it will make for a very expensive ride. The first half hour of each ride is free, the next half hour costs €1 and from there it gets continuously more expensive. Vélib' is cheapest for short rides. Kids aged two to eight can also take advantage of the bike-share program with P'tit Vélib'. You'll find these kids' bikes in select spots, including Berges de Seine, the Bois de Boulogne, and Canal de l'Ourcq.

Guided **bike tours** in Paris are increasing in popularity. Numerous bike stores rent bikes, and tours are offered by companies such as Holland Bikes *(www.hollandbikes.com)*, Paris Bike Tour *(www.parisbiketour.net)*, and Paris à Vélo c'est Sympa! *(www.parisvelosympa.com)*.

1 Go for a romantic dinner on the terrace at **Minipalais**. > p. 110

2 Dine in the bedroom or by the ping-pong table at **Le Derrière.** > p. 66

3 Enjoy the nice terrace at **Le Saut du Loup** in the Tuileries. > p. 49

4 Order typical French fare at **Bouillon Chartier.** > p. 46

5 Join the locals for a healthy lunch at the hip **Café Pinson.** > p. 70

6 Savor exquisite French cuisine at **Le Chateaubriand.** > p. 126

7 Dine under a glass ceiling at **Le Dôme du Marais.** > p. 70

8 Enjoy the best pita bread in Paris at **Miznon** in the Marais. > p. 69

9 Splurge and enjoy the amazing view at the hip **Georges.** > p. 66

10 Eat in a secret courtyard at **Hôtel Particulier Montmartre.** > 23 Avenue Junot Pavillon D 18th arr.

TOP 10 | SHOPPING

1 Dance under the bridge next to the Seine at **Faust.** > p. 110

2 Go local at **Brasserie Barbès.** > 2 Boulevard Barbès 18th arr.

3 Enjoy jazz at **Sunset-Sunside.** > 60 Rue des Lombards 1st arr.

4 Sip cocktails in style at **Kong.** > 1 Rue du Pont Neuf 1st arr.

5 Party outside at **Wanderlust.** > 32 Quai d Austerlitz 13th arr.

6 Experience an artistic night out at **La Bellevilloise.** > p. 134

7 Discover the dance clubs near **La Machine du Moulin Rouge.** > 90 Boulevard de Clichy 18th arr.

8 Catch a French flick at **Cinéma Studio 28.** > p. 34

9 Enjoy a concert at **Studio de l'Ermitage.** > p. 133

10 Listen to DJ music at alternative **Bar Ourq.** > p. 125

TOP 10 | SUNDAY

1 Start the day with breakfast and a macaron at **Ladurée.** > p. 116

2 Take a trip to the local market **Marché Aligre** and drink wine at **Le Baron Rouge.** > p. 142

3 Enjoy brunch at **Le Marché des Enfants Rouges.** > p. 77

4 Stroll along the **Canal St.-Martin.** > p. 134

5 Visit the flea market **Marché aux Puces de St.-Ouen.** > p. 138

6 Up for an exhibit? Go to **MEP,** a photography museum. > p. 65

7 Take a coffee and cake break at **Le Loir dans la Théière.** > p. 69

8 Sip an *apéro* (aperitif) outside at **Café de Flore.** > p. 89

9 Have a rooftop drink at **Le Perchoir.** > p. 129

10 Head to **Au Lapin Agile** for a fun night of French music. > p. 34

WALK **1**

BATIGNOLLES & MONTMARTRE

ABOUT THE WALK

This walk takes you through the 17th (Batignolles) and 18th (Montmartre) arrondissements. The beginning of the walk through Batignolles is particularly interesting if you've already been to Paris a few times and want to check out an up-and-coming residential neighborhood with nice shops and hip restaurants. Otherwise, if it's your first time in Paris, start at number 6 and visit the artist neighborhood of Montmartre.

THE NEIGHBORHOODS

More and more young families are moving to Batignolles and hanging out in the hip local restaurants. The nicest part of the neighborhood is between the market hall and the **Parc des Batignolles,** where there are lots of shops and cafés. Regular activities, such as antique markets, are organized around the park.

La butte (the hill) of Montmartre, in the 18th arrondissement, stands out high above its surroundings. A century ago this neighborhood—with its winding streets and amazing panoramas—was still just a village outside Paris. In the late 19th century numerous artists settled here, including Cézanne, Van Gogh, Renoir, and Toulouse-Lautrec, who immortalized the local nightlife in his artwork. Today Montmartre continues to attract creative souls, and many painters, photographers, directors, and journalists live in the neighborhood. You can get a taste of this at **Place du Tertre.** To visit the top of the hill you'll have to walk up and down small streets, but the reward at the top is worth it. The view from **Sacré-Cœur,** the highest point in Paris, is spectacular.

The diversity of shops and cafés makes Montmartre particularly pleasant. Street musicians at **Place des Abbesses,** the non-touristy heart of the neighborhood, add to the charming atmosphere. The beautiful architecture on **Avenue Junot** and **Villa Léandre** also contribute to its unique character. Lots of the local

Clignancourt porcelain and a wonderful assortment of posters from the golden age of Montmartre.

12-14 rue cortot, 18th arr., www.museedemontmartre.fr, t: 0149258939, open daily mid sept-mid may 10am-6pm, mid may-mid sept 10am-7pm, entrance €9.50, metro lamarck caulaincourt

(21) The Roman-Byzantine **Sacré-Cœur** Basilica was built to honor the Sacred Heart of Jesus and ask forgiveness for the blood shed during the Franco-Prussian War and the revolutionary rule of the Paris Commune that followed. Thanks to nationwide fundraising, building began in 1876. Today the basilica houses a trove of valuable objects. The view over Paris from the stairs out front is priceless.

35 rue du chevalier de la barre, 18th arr., www.sacre-coeur-montmartre.com, t: 0153418900, open daily 6am-10:30pm, free entrance, metro abbesses

(33) In the 16th century, Montmartre was characterized by its many windmills, used to grind wheat and press grapes. Unfortunately, only a very few of these windmills remain today, one of which is **Le Moulin de la Galette.** You can get a nice meal in the restaurant now located there.

83 rue lepic, 18th arr., www.lemoulindelagalette.fr, t: 0146068477, open daily noon-11pm, metro blanche/abbesses

(34) Marcel Aymé is the author of the novel *Le Passe-Muraille,* which tells the story of a man who can walk through walls. Artist Jean Marais drew inspiration from this book when he created the statue **Passe-Muraille.**

place marcel aymé, 18th arr., metro abbesses/lamarck caulaincourt

FOOD & DRINK

(2) Brunch at **Les Puces des Batignolles** is so popular that the restaurant had to open a second location across the street. The brunch includes a sweet basket with croissants and jam, and a savory main course with a burger and/or eggs, plus coffee, tea, or fresh juice. Everything is served on playful, colorful dishes.

110 rue legendre, 17th arr., t: 0142266226, open mon-fri 8am-2pm, sat-sun 10am-2pm, price €18, metro rome/brochant

③ **Le Club des Cinq** is popular among the neighborhood yuppies, who like to come here for lunch or dinner. The restaurant is full of wonderfully colorful decorations, and the walls are covered with pictures of comic strip characters. It gets its name from *The Famous Five,* a popular kids' book series by British author Enid Blyton. Order the cheeseburger or the salmon burger—both are delicious!

57 rue des batignolles, 17th arr., www.leclubdes5.fr, t: 0153049473, open mon-sun 7:30pm-10:30pm, tue-fri noon-2:30pm, sat-sun noon-4pm, price €16, metro rome/brochant

④ **Les Caves Populaires** is an inviting neighborhood café, particularly popular among students. Order a cheese platter and a glass of wine, and have a nice chat with the people around you.

22 rue des dames, 17th arr., t: 0153040832, open mon-sat 8am-2am, sun 11am-2am, price €10, metro rome/place de clichy

⑦ The **Terrass Hotel** was fully renovated in 2015. The seventh floor is now a restaurant offering an amazing panoramic view over the city from inside and out on the terrace. You can reserve a table inside on the website, but they don't take reservations for the terrace.

12-14 rue joseph de maistre, 18th arr., www.terrass-hotel.com, t: 0146067285, open daily: bar 11am-11pm, lunch noon-2pm, dinner 7pm-10pm, price 2-course lunch €24, dinner main course € 25, metro blanche/abbesses

⑨ **Café des Deux Moulins'** popularity has skyrocketed since the success of the film *Amélie.* Order a *crème brûlée d'Amélie* and a cup of coffee on the terrace.

15 rue lepic, 18th arr., t: 0142549050, open daily 7:30am-1am, price set lunch €14.90 or €17.90, metro blanche

⑭ **Marcel** is a New York-style café on the corner of the beautiful street Villa Léandre. The menu primarily offers British and American dishes such as eggs Benedict and blueberry pancakes. This small, dark, but good restaurant is enormously popular among local hipsters. The café has a number of locations in other popular areas around the city as well.

1 villa leandre, 18th arr., www.restaurantmarcel.fr, t: 0146060404, open mon-fri 10am-11pm, brunch sat-sun 10am-7pm, price €23, metro lamarck coulaincourt

⑲ Everything on the menu at **Soul Kitchen** is organic. Try a freshly baked muffin, a slice of cheesecake, or a delicious cup of soup. Each morning around 11:00am they write the day's menu on a chalkboard. The options are always healthy and the price always good. Get the Mexican chocolate milk, grab a game off the shelf, and stay for the afternoon.
33 rue lamarck, 18th arr., fb: soulkitchenparis, t: 0171379995, open tue-fri 8:30am-6.30pm, sat-sun 10am-7pm, price €15, metro lamarck caulaincourt

㉒ As you head down the steps from Sacré-Cœur, an inviting terrace with colorful tables suddenly appears from behind the trees. **L'Été en Pente Douce** is a great place for a break and just off the beaten tourist path.
23 rue muller, 18th arr., t: 0142640267, open daily noon-midnight, price €17.50, metro anvers

㉕ The retro-industrial rock-'n'-roll bar **La Fourmi** is known as a place where bands like to warm up before taking the stage at nearby concert hall La Cigale. It can get really busy here after performances. Grab some flyers from the bar to see what's happening in the neighborhood. This is mainly a place for drinks, although the menu does offer sandwiches and salads if you're hungry.
74 rue des martyrs, 18th arr., t: 0142647035, open sun-thu 8am-2am, fri-sat 8am-4am, metro pigalle

㉚ Bakery, pastry shop and restaurant in one—**Coquelicot** has something for every time of the day. Perfect for brunch, lunch, or snack time. Tip: This is a perfect place to put together a delicious picnic basket.
24 rue des abbesses, 18th arr., www.coquelicot-montmartre.com, t: 0146061877, open bakery tue-sun 7:30am-8pm, restaurant tue-fri 8am-5:30pm, sat-sun 8am-6:30pm, price brunch €18.45, metro abbesses/pigalle

㉛ The French owner of **Aloy Aloy** is married to a Thai woman, and they run this restaurant together. Fun family photos on the wall give the place an intimate feel, and their award-winning *bo bun* was chosen as the best in Paris. You'll come across many more great restaurants as you head downhill.
61 rue des trois frères, 18th arr., t: 0142558977, open tue-fri 7:30pm-11pm, sat-sun noon-1:30pm & 7:30pm-11pm, price €15.50, metro abbesses

③② From the moment it opened, the chic bistro **Le Coq Rico** has been a huge success. As the name suggests, the menu revolves around poultry. Try the delectable chicken soup or the French chicken livers, or spring for a whole *rôti* chicken from the oven to share. They also serve of variety of egg dishes, all prepared from organic and locally sourced eggs.

98 rue lepic, 18th arr., www.lecoqrico.com, t: 0142598289, open daily noon-2:30pm & 7pm-11pm, price chicken to share €85, lunch €15, metro abbesses

SHOPPING

① The **Marché couvert Batignolles** is a covered market where you'll find a plethora of French products, including vegetables, cheeses, meats, fish, etc. Be sure to stop by the Iranian stand in the middle of the market. Their olive-fig tapenade is unparalleled and they'll even give you a sample to prove it.

96 bis rue lemercier, 17th arr., t: 0148859330, open tue-fri 8:30am-1pm & 3:30pm-8pm, sun 8:30am-8pm, sun 8:30am-2pm, metro brochant

⑧ **Tombées du Camion** is French for "things that fell off the truck." This shop is chock full of curious and unusual objects. Most items—billiard balls, doll eyes, badges, jewelry, tins, and bags of spices—are old and unused and will transport you back to the 1930s and 40s. The bins full of meticulously sorted rarities make this shop a place you'll definitely want to discover.

17 rue joseph de maistre, 18th arr., www.tombeesducamion.com, t: 0981216280, open daily 1pm-8pm, metro abbesses/blanche

⑪ At **L'Atelier,** you can purchase a pair of shoes designed by a team of two brothers. They make the shoes themselves in the workshop under the store, where the floor is strewn with leather remnants in a rainbow of colors. Choose the design you want, along with the color and type of leather, and within three weeks you'll have your own unique pair of shoes.

58 rue lepic, 18th arr., www.chaussures-latelier.com, t: 0142239661, open tue-fri 11am-1pm & 3:15pm-7:15pm, sat 11am-1pm & 3:15pm-6:30pm, metro abbesses/blanche

peep-toe

Richelieu

scarpin

MOCASSIN

bottine

Shoes

(12) The owner of the colorful collection at **Orpiment** selects all the clothes and accessories for sale herself. Hats, bags, dresses, scarves, jewelry, and gloves—everything is chosen with the utmost care and attention.
46 rue caulaincourt, 18th arr., t: 0142546729, open tue & thu-sat 11:30am-8pm, wed 5pm-8pm, metro place de clichy

(24) **Marché St.-Pierre** is the most famous fabric market in Paris. Enter through Dreyfus Déballage and prepare to be amazed at the enormous selection you find. Be sure to also take a look across the street at Tissus Reine on Place St.-Pierre. The mini mannequins throughout the store show off the latest fabric trends.
2 rue charles nodier, 18th arr., www.marchesaintpierre.com, t: 0146069225, open mon-fri 10am-6:30pm, sat 10am-7pm, metro anvers

(26) Once you set eyes on the colorful, feminine dresses at **Héroines** you'll have no choice but to go in and check out the store. They have small sizes for little ladies and dresses that will steal the show at any party. The accessories are also worth checking out—shoes, feminine cufflinks and leather belts in a variety of colors.
7 rue des abbesses, 18th arr., www.boutiques-heroines.com, t: 0967072104, open daily 11am-8pm, metro abbesses

(27) In Rue la Vieuville you'll find a number of nice shops, including **Spree.** You'll find the newest collections from designers such as Vanessa Bruno, Isabel Marant, and Tsumori Chisato. Check out the great selection of retro furniture, too.
16 rue la vieuville, 18th arr., www.spree.fr, t: 0142234140, open tue-sat 11am-7pm, sun 3pm-7pm, metro abbesses

(29) Marie Rose Guarnieri's bookstore **Librairie des Abbesses** is something of an institution in Montmartre. It is also one of the last cultural havens in the neighborhood, which is now primarily dominated by clothing shops. The store hosts regular readings and book presentations.
30 rue yvonne le tac, 18th arr., www.librairiedesabbesses.blogspot.com, t: 0146068430, open mon 11am-8pm, tue-fri 9:30am-8pm, sat 10am-8pm, sun noon-8pm, metro abbesses

MORE TO EXPLORE

⑤ **LE BAL**—one of the hottest spots in the neighborhood—was a dancehall in the 1920s. Today it holds an exhibition space where modern photographers and video artists display their work, and a store with unique art books. On the weekends, the modern café serves English-style brunch.

6 impasse de la defense, 18th arr., www.le-bal.fr, t: 0144707550, open wed & fri noon-8pm, thu noon-10pm, sat 11am-8pm, sun 11am-7pm, entrance €6, metro place de clichy

⑩ Pop inside **Cinéma Studio 28** to see what's showing. This local movie theater dates back to the end of the 19th century and maintains much of its original character today. Artists such as Jean Cocteau and André Breton even held performances here in the past. When the weather is nice, the patio is a pleasant place for a break.

10 rue tholozé, 18th arr., www.cinemastudio28.com, t: 0146063607, see website for opening hours, entrance €9, metro abbesses/blanche

⑯ What goes on in this beautiful house, behind the pink facade and green shutters? Every evening, starting at 9pm, **Au Lapin Agile** features live cabaret shows. Local artists sing an array of French chansons and transport you back to the Montmartre of yesteryear. For fans of French music, Au Lapin Agile is not to be missed.

22 rue des saules, 18th arr., www.au-lapin-agile.com, t: 0146068587, open tue-sun 9pm-1am, entrance €28, metro abbesses/lamarck caulaincourt

⑳ Montmartre was once much-loved by poets and painters alike. Perhaps that's why the busy, touristy **Place du Tertre** is nowadays always swarming with so-called artists wanting to draw your portrait. The souvenir shops and cafés on the square are also eager to cash in on the area's rich artistic past.

place du tertre, 18th arr., metro abbesses

㉓ In the 19th century, the **Halle St.-Pierre** was the center of the fabric trade. Now the beautiful glass and metal building houses the Musée d'Art Brut et d'Art Singulier. You can come here to see temporary exhibits, take a workshop, or

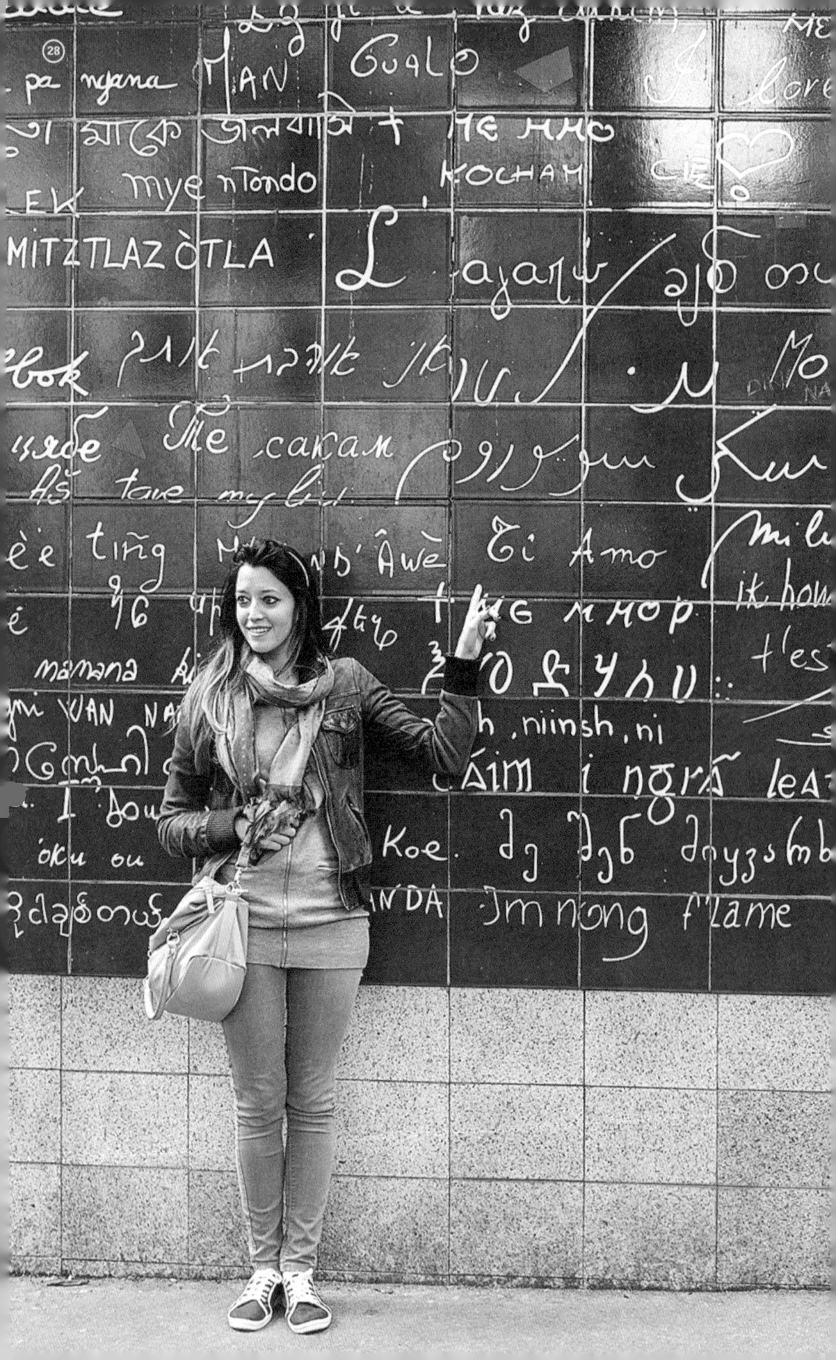

mye nTondo
KOCHAM
MITZTLAZ ÒTLA
Ti Amo
.niinsh.ni
Koe
mamana

simply read the paper and have a bite in the charming café. Be sure to stop in at the bookshop—it has beautiful postcards.

2 rue ronsard, 18th arr., www.hallesaintpierre.org, t: 0142587289, open mon-fri 11am-6pm, sat 11am-7pm, sun noon-6pm, free entrance to gallery, temporary exhibits €9, metro anvers

㉘ Behind Place des Abbesses, in a small public garden on Square Jehan-Rictus, you'll find **Le Mur des je t'aime.** The wall, created in 2000, displays the phrase "I love you" 311 times in languages and dialects from around the world. You might have to look closely, but you'll find English on there somewhere.

place des abbesses, 18th arr., www.lesjetaime.com, open mon-fri 8am-8:30pm, sat-sun 9am-8:30pm, metro abbesses

WALK **2**

QUARTIER DES MARTYRS, GRANDS BOULEVARDS, LOUVRE & MADELEINE

ABOUT THE WALK

This walk takes you to Paris's Right Bank, namely the 9th, 1st, and 2nd arrondissements. The walk is a mix of shopping and culture. In Rue des Martyrs and the shopping arcades you can go window shopping and more. Along the way there are small museums, the Palais Royal gardens, and the Louvre where you can take in art and culture. The route starts right under Montmartre and descends toward the Seine, so don't do it in reverse or you'll be in for a lot of uphill walking.

THE NEIGHBORHOODS

The 9th arrondissement, the northern neighborhood between Notre-Dame de Lorette, Trinité, and Place Pigalle, has been called the **"golden artists' triangle."** In the second half of the 19th century, it was the preferred neighborhood for artists and intellectuals such as Sand, Delacroix, and Chopin. This area of the city is known for its classic architecture, with *hôtels particuliers* (grand residences), charming squares, quiet courtyards, and small museums. The **Rue des Martyrs** is the best-known street in the neighborhood. Here you'll find a variety of stores along with nice places to eat and drink. On Sundays, this is a great area to come to for brunch among the locals.

The **Rive Droite** (Right Bank) and the **Grands Boulevards** feature many fancy shopping arcades, such as Galerie Vivienne. These arcades date back to the first half of the 19th century and were built to protect the wealthy from the elements while shopping. There are also large department stores on the Grands Boulevards, including Galeries Lafayette and Le Printemps. Around the square where the enormous Roman temple La Madeleine is located are numerous specialty food stores and tea rooms.

WALK 2 DESCRIPTION (approx. 5.1 miles)

Start at Métro Blanche and head downhill on Rue Blanche. Take the third street to the left, Rue Chaptal, for a romantic experience ❶. Turn on Rue Henner and then go left on Rue de la Bruyère. Halfway down the street, take a detour to the right for another museum ❷. Afterwards, continue to the traffic light. Cross the street and head down Rue Henry Monnier ❸ ❹ ❺. Turn on Rue Clauzel and take the first street on your left ❻ ❼. After Rue des Martyrs bends, turn down Avenue Trudaine ❽. Take a right on Rue de Rochechouart. Just down the second street on the left is a nice lunch spot ❾. Continue past the end of Rue de Rochechouart and down to Métro Cadet. Along the way you'll pass a number of nice stores ❿. At Métro Cadet, cross the street and continue on Rue Cadet. Cross Rue du Faubourg Montmartre, go a little to the left and then turn right almost immediately into Passage Jouffroy Verdeau ⓫. Walk through the passage until you get to Boulevard de Montmartre. Take a left here and then another left for a classic restaurant ⓬, or cross the Boulevard and head into the Passage des Panoramas ⓭. Walk through the passage toward Rue Vivienne and have bread with chocolate spread for lunch ⓮. Afterwards, continue straight until you see the entrance to Galerie Vivienne on your left ⓯. Walk through the shopping arcade. When you exit, cross Rue des Petits Champs and turn to the left, continuing straight on Rue la Feuillade to Place des Victoires ⓰. Walk back to Rue des Petits Champs and turn left after you pass Galerie Vivienne. Enter the Jardin du Palais Royal ⓱ and walk through the beautiful garden to the exit on the other side at Place du Palais Royal. Cross Rue de Rivoli here toward the Louvre ⓲ ⓳. Walk along the right side of the Louvre gardens for a museum and a nice terrace ⓴ ㉑. Instead of going into the Tuileries gardens, turn right on Rue des Pyramides. Take the first left on Rue St.-Honoré ㉒. Turn right, towards Place du Marché St.-Honoré ㉓. Continue straight down Rue d'Antin until Avenue de l'Opéra, and cross the street. Take a left on Rue Monsigny ㉔. Turn left again on Rue du Quatre Septembre until you get to the Opéra ㉕. Beyond this point are large department stores on Boulevard Haussmann ㉖. Head down Rue Scribe until Boulevard des Capucines. Along the way you'll pass a perfume museum ㉗. Cross to the other side of the boulevard and go right ㉘. Continue straight until the church ㉙. Walk around the church ㉚ ㉛ ㉜ to arrive at two recommended restaurants, where you can end the day on a delicious note ㉝ ㉞.

SIGHTS & ATTRACTIONS

(1) The building that now houses the **Musée de la Vie Romantique** was a meeting place for Paris's Romantic artists during the 19th century. This *hôtel particulier* was the home and studio of painter Ary Scheffer. His works tell us all about this time period, as does memorabilia of writer George Sand. The tea room and the idyllic garden are especially romantic.

16 rue chaptal, 9th arr., t: 0155319567, open tue-sun 10am-6pm, tea garden april-oct, free entrance to permanent collection, temporary exhibits starting at €7, metro blanche

(2) Artist Gustave Moreau (1826-1898) was considered part of the Symbolism movement. His former home and studio now houses the **Musée National Gustave Moreau.** His unique paintings cover the walls from floor to ceiling, and numerous sketches and watercolors are displayed in glass cases.

14 rue de la rochefoucauld, 9th arr., www.musee-moreau.fr, t: 0148743850, open mon & wed-thu 10am-12:45pm & 2pm-5:15pm, fri-sun 10am-5:15pm, entrance €6, metro trinité/st.-georges

(18) The building that is home to the **Musée du Louvre** has served many purposes—from medieval fortress to imperial palace. In 1793 Napoleon decided to open the palace to the public, and the Louvre has since become the richest, most visited museum in the world. There is so much to see that even if you were to just fleetingly glance at all the artwork here, it would still take you a full day or two. Tip: Avoid the lines and buy your tickets online.

34-36 quai du louvre, 1st arr., www.louvre.fr, t: 0140205317, open sat-mon & thu 9am-6pm, wed & fri 9am-9:45pm, entrance €16.60, metro palais royal/musée du louvre

(20) Applied art is the focus of the **Musée des Arts Décoratifs:** interior and graphic design, advertising, and fashion. The permanent collection includes interesting Art Nouveau and Art Deco pieces, and modern furniture from the 20th century. The museum also has temporary exhibits. The view out over the Jardin des Tuileries from the top floor of the building is amazing.

107-111 rue de rivoli, 1st arr., www.lesartsdecoratifs.fr, t: 0144555750, open tue-wed & fri-sun 11am-6pm, thu 11am-9pm, entrance €11, metro palais royal/musée du louvre

㉕ **L'Opéra Garnier** was built between 1862 and 1875. The "wedding cake"—as the building is affectionately known—was designed by Charles Garnier. The opulent edifice features a mix of styles and is adorned with hundreds of statues. During the day, tours of the building are offered. The best option, however, is to see a performance there.

8 rue scribe, 9th arr., www.operadeparis.fr, t: 0144615965, open daily 10am-5pm, entrance €7, audio guide and multimedia tour €5/hour (€12 with ipad), metro opéra

㉗ The French are known to be proud of their products. So it's not surprising that there is an entire museum dedicated to Fragonard, a perfumery from the southern town of Grasse, known for its flowery fragrances. **Musée Fragonard** is located in a beautiful old building that dates back to 1860, and much of the museum's decoration reflects that time period. A multilingual guide will give you a tour and you can check out a private perfume collection. Extend the olfactory pleasure beyond your visit and buy your favorite fragrance to take home.

9 rue scribe, 9th arr., www.fragonard.com, t: 0147420456, open mon-sat 9am-6pm, sun 9am-5pm, free entrance, metro opéra

㉙ With **La Madeleine,** Napoleon had wanted to construct a Roman temple honoring the glory of his army. Building began in 1764, but by the time it was finished in 1842, there was no longer need for a monument to celebrate Napoleon's fallen soldiers. The building was converted to a church where they hold a daily mass.

place de la madeleine, 8th arr., www.eglise-lamadeleine.com, t: 0144516900, open daily 9:30am-7pm, free entrance, metro madeleine

FOOD & DRINK

⑤ At Place Gustave Toudouze, you can relax and take a break at any of the various terraces. Locals come here on the weekend, in part because it's a great place to enjoy the sun, but also to see and be seen. **No Stress Café** has nice outdoor seating and lots of inviting places to sit inside too.

2 place gustave toudouze, 9th arr., t: 0148780027, open daily 11am-2am, price set lunch €13, metro st.-georges

(6) The restaurant at the small, chic **Hôtel Amour** is a good place to come for a drink, lunch, or a romantic dinner. With a little luck, you can get a spot in the pleasant inner courtyard. They serve a delicious brunch on the weekends.
8 rue de navarin, 9th arr., www.hotelamourparis.fr, t: 0148783180, open mon-sat noon-midnight, sun noon-5pm, price €33, brunch €26, metro pigalle/st.-georges

(7) From the day it first opened, **Le Pantruche** has been hugely popular—and for good reason. Classic, refined French cuisine is served with originality and professionalism. The interior is simple yet stylish, and the quality is perfect for the price. The restaurant is unfortunately only open on weekdays.
3 rue victor massé, 9th arr, www.lepantruche.com, t: 0148785560, open mon-fri 12:30pm-2:30pm & 7:30pm-10:30pm, price lunch €18, dinner €34, metro pigalle/st.-georges

(8) On Rue des Martyrs and Avenue Trudaine there are a variety of restaurants where you can go for a nice bite to eat. Want something special? Head to the Hungarian restaurant **Le Paprika,** which is known for its delicious goulash. Prefer to stick with local fare? That's okay too—they also have French dishes on the menu.
28 avenue trudaine, 9th arr., www.le-paprika.com, t: 0144630291, open daily 10am-11:30pm, price €20, metro pigalle/anvers

(9) Every time you set foot inside **Cornercafé Apatam,** you'll notice that the Belgian chef and his French wife have added a new bit of decoration. The café feels like a colorful living room. Sink into one of the armchairs that come from the second-hand store next door, and settle in for a couple hours of dining pleasure. On Thursday and Friday nights they serve one set menu, put together by the chef. Reservations are a must.
10 rue thimonnier, 9th arr., www.cornercafe.fr, t: 0177160144, open mon-wed noon-2pm, thu-fri noon-2pm & 8pm-10pm, price set meal €33, metro anvers

(12) The legendary **Bouillon Chartier** has been around since 1896 and is something of an institution in Paris. The restaurant's concept has always remained the same: good food for a good price, served up with outstanding service. Today, it is still as popular as ever. They don't take reservations, so the line out front

continuously grows as the evening progresses. Tip: Come here for an early dinner, and you're likely to be seated immediately. The extensive menu offers a variety of typical French dishes, and the large dining area—with lots of glass and mirrors—is a historic monument. The restaurant is definitely worth the visit.

7 rue du faubourg montmartre, 9th arr., www.bouillon-chartier.com, t: 0147708629, open daily 11:30am-10pm, price €15, metro grands boulevards

⑬ **L'Arbre à Cannelle** is a great spot in the Passage des Panoramas. The wooden decor gives the place an inviting feel. Everything—the tables, the chairs and even the ceiling—is made of wood. This restaurant/tea room is known for its sweet and savory tarts, such as the chocolate-tangerine tart, and the house crumble.

57 passage des panoramas, 2nd arr., www.passagedespanoramas.fr, t: 0145085587, open mon-sat noon-3pm & 7pm-11pm, price lunch €23, metro grands boulevards

⑭ **Le Pain de la Bourse** is a good spot for breakfast or lunch next to the beautiful Paris Stock Exchange. Slide into a seat at one of the long wooden tables. They serve baskets filled with a variety of breads that you can top with, among other treats, three types of homemade chocolate spreads—white, dark, and hazelnut. The concept was imported from Belgium, and Parisians are hooked. Locals love to come here for weekend brunch.

33 rue vivienne, 2nd arr., t: 0142367602, open mon-sat 8am-10pm, sun 8am-6pm, price €15, metro bourse

⑲ At **Café Marly,** enjoy a bit of luxury as you sit in the arcade of the royal palace and look out over the Louvre courtyard and I.M. Pei's famous glass pyramid. This is a great spot for lunch.

93 rue de rivoli, 1st arr., www.cafe-marly.com, t: 0149260660, open daily 8am-2am, price €25, metro palais royal/musée du louvre

㉑ Outdoor seating at modern restaurant **Le Saut du Loup** lies just beyond the throngs of tourists that stream through the Jardin des Tuileries. It's perfect for a delicious, elegant lunch and offers diners a view out over the gardens. The seats are in the sun, but there are plenty of patio umbrellas if you prefer a little shade. From the terrace, the Eiffel Tower is visible in the distance. Perfect for a romantic date!

107 rue de rivoli, 1st arr., www.lesautduloup.fr, t: 0142254955, open daily noon-10pm, price €23, metro louvre rivoli/tuileries

㉓ There are a variety of places to eat at the Place du Marché de St.-Honoré, from simple to stylish. One of the more upscale places is **L'Absinthe.** The food here is great: beautiful fish and meat dishes served in a classic, charming interior.

24 place du marché st.-honoré, 1st arr., www.restaurantabsinthe.com, t: 0149269004, open mon-thu noon-2:15pm & 7pm-10:15pm, fri noon-2:15pm & 7pm-10:45pm, sat 7pm-10:45pm, price €22, metro tuileries

㉔ **Habemus** is popular among Parisians who work in this neighborhood. Not only is it always hopping at lunch, but it's busy at happy hour, too. Mix with the locals and enjoy a good meal. Nearby, the arcade Passage Choiseuil has lots of shops to check out.

13 rue monsigny, 2nd arr., www.habemus-restaurant.fr, t: 0147429235, open mon-fri noon-3pm & 6:30pm-2am, sat 6:30pm-2am, price €17, metro pyramides/opéra/quatre septembre

㉝ To get to **Le Village,** leave the crowds near la Madeleine behind and head into Village Royal. This charming passageway between Rue Royal and Rue Boissy d'Anglas is like a small town in the middle of the big city. Parisians who work in the neighborhood come here for a quick bite. It has a great terrace that is heated in winter. This is a nice place to sit, but don't expect a top-quality dining experience.

25 rue royale, 8th arr., t: 0140170219, open mon-sat 8am-7pm, price €25, metro madeleine

㉞ Have you ever eaten in a restaurant where you can order a glass of wine from literally every wine-producing country in the world, even a Dutch wine from the southern province of Limburg? You can at **Le Taste Monde.** Owner Sylvain has traveled the world and hand-picked all of the wines. If you find it too overwhelming to choose from the 900 wines on offer, let one of the wine

experts here help you. Between 3:00pm and 7:00pm, the wine cellar is open as a store. Tip: The 3-course meal of the day is cheaper before 8:00pm.

8 rue de surène, 8th arr., www.letastemonde.com, t: 0142661989, open mon-wed noon-2pm & 7pm-10pm, thu-fri noon-2pm & 7pm-11pm, sat 7pm-11pm, price 3-course meal €43, until 8pm €27, metro madeleine

SHOPPING

③ **Pois Plume** is a cute shop for the tiniest tots and their parents. They have clothes, decorations for the baby's room and toys. The collection has been very carefully put together, and the colors, fabrics and clothes will bring a smile to your face. You might not be able to leave without a cute little something for someone.

4 rue henry monnier, 9th arr, www.poisplume.com, t: 0148743938, open tue-sat 11am-7pm, sun 1pm-6pm, metro st.-georges

④ How **Juju s'amuse** manages time and again to put together such a great clothing collection is a mystery. But it does, and after opening three stores in Paris, Juju now also has a shop in New York. The store offers colorful, original items for the fashion-conscious lady.

3 rue henry monnier, 9th arr., www.jujusamuse.com, open mon-sat 11am-8pm, sun 11:30am-1:30pm, metro st.-georges

⑩ **Le Jupon Rouge** is a mix of refurbished furniture, vintage clothes, shoes, and bags. The vibe is cool and feminine. It's a local shop where women from the neighborhood love to stop by. They take the time to look around or chat with owner Marie and give her orange cat Icare a little scratch behind the ears. Who knows, maybe you'll find a nice pair of second-hand Dior shoes for a good price.

18 rue de rochechouart, 9th arr., t: 0148785454, open mon 2:30pm-7pm, tue-sat 11am-1pm & 2:30pm-7pm, metro cadet

⑪ At **La Boîte à Joujoux** you can find anything you might need to make your doll house complete. This is a world of miniatures for the true hobbyist, or for anyone who wants to be surprised by just how many things are available in mini.

41 passage jouffroy, 9th arr., www.joujoux.com, t: 0148245837, open mon-sat 10am-7pm, metro grands boulevards

(22) **Colette** is the number one concept store in Paris. Everything here is modern—the staff, the clientele, the merchandise, and the interior. Items are displayed as if in a gallery. The restaurant is a good place for lunch.

213 rue st.-honoré, 1st arr., www.colette.fr, t: 0155353390, open mon-sat 11am-7pm, metro tuileries

(26) The large department stores collectively referred to as **Les Grands Magasins** are all right next to each other. The most well-known is Galeries Lafayette, with its beautiful glass and metal dome. Less touristy is Le Printemps. Le Citadium, behind Le Printemps, sells the latest styles in streetwear.

40 boulevard haussman, 9th arr., www.galerieslafayette.com, t: 0142823456, open mon-wed & fri-sat 9:30am-8pm, thu 9:30am-9pm, metro chaussée d'antin la fayette

(28) **Lavinia** has a large selection of wines and is a nice place to stop for a break. Let the salespeople tell you about their wines and then pick out a bottle to try. Bring the bottle right from the store upstairs to the tasting bar and terrace. You just pay the store's ticket price for the bottle you choose. Of course, you can also wait until you get home to pop the cork.

3-5 boulevard de la madeleine, 9th arr., www.lavinia.fr, t: 014297202, open mon-sat store 10am-8:30pm, restaurant noon-9pm, metro madeleine

(30) You'll find the most luxurious tasty treats at **Fauchon,** founded in 1886. They have countless gourmet items, a heavenly cake shop, a tea room, a deli, and a wine cellar.

24-26 & 30 place de la madeleine, 8th arr., www.fauchon.com, t: 0170393800, open cake shop and bakery mon-sat 9am-8pm, café open daily 8am-8:30pm, metro madeleine

(31) **La Maison de la Truffe** smells of truffles, the expensive mushrooms that grow underground. In the restaurant, you can order dishes such as an omelet

with truffle slices, and the store offers products such as truffle-infused olive oil, truffle *risotto,* and even chocolate with truffles.

19 place de la madeleine, 8th arr., www.maison-de-la-truffe.com, t: 0142655322, store open mon-sat 10am-10pm, restaurant mon-sat noon-10:30pm, metro madeleine

㉜ Since 1747, **Maille** has been about one product: mustard. Here you'll find the most unique flavors and colors of mustard—from traditional mustard with honey or nuts, to red mustard with berries and green mustard with herbs. They also have a nice selection of oils and vinegars made with mustard. You can buy jarred mustard, or bring your own container and have it filled fresh from the pump. This true French product is a great compliment to many of the other delicious French treats that you can buy around La Madeleine.

6 place de la madeleine, 8th arr., www.maille.com, t: 0140150600, open mon-sat 10am-7pm, metro madeleine

MORE TO EXPLORE

⑮ Paris is full of shopping arcades. The glass-covered halls were built during the 19th century under the supervision of the architect Georges-Eugène Haussmann, who was likely inspired by the architecture of Arabian souks. The best preserved and perhaps liveliest of these arcades is **Galerie Vivienne,** built in 1823 and decorated in Empire style.

5 rue de la banque, 4 rue des petits-champs, 6 rue vivienne, 2nd arr., www.galerie-vivienne.com, open daily 9am-8pm, metro bourse

⑯ **Place des Victoires** is a forgotten place in Paris. This round square offers a respite from the crowds of tourists. A number of famous fashion brands have stores here, so there is good shopping to be done. The square was built in 1684 to encircle a statue of Louis XIV. The statue has been destroyed on numerous occasions, but has been replaced every time.

place des victoires, 2nd arr., metro bourse/sentier

⑰ Since 1986, Daniel Buren's black and white columns have been adding a bit of extra pep to the stately palace garden **Jardin du Palais Royal,** delivering a surprising contrast between old and new. Nearby shopping arcades house a variety of stores. Head to Serge Lutens for perfume, Stella McCartney for feminine clothes with a British twist, Pierre Hardy for high-fashion shoes, and Journal Standard de Luxe for good-looking basics. Along the way, stop at any of the fantastic terraces and soak up the Parisian vibe.

2 place colette, 1st arr., palais-royal.monuments-nationaux.fr, t: 0147039216, open daily oct-march 7am-8:30pm, april-may 7am-10:15pm, june-aug 7am-11pm, sept 7am-9:30pm, free entrance, metro palais royal/musée du louvre

WALK 3

LES HALLES & LE MARAIS

ABOUT THE WALK

This walk is on the Right Bank and takes you through the 1st, 3rd, and 4th arrondissements. The walk is not ideal for Saturdays, when many of the stores and restaurants in this traditionally Jewish neighborhood are closed. Stop regularly at sidewalk cafés and take in everything around you. It's easy to spend an entire day here walking around and enjoying all of the hidden streets, unexpected squares, sidewalk cafés, and interesting shops.

THE NEIGHBORHOODS

Les Halles and the Marais are adjoining neighborhoods on the Right Bank. Les Halles was previously home to the city's largest covered market, as well as locally beloved restaurants. In 1969 some of the merchants moved to the suburbs and the market was torn down. In 1979 it was replaced with an underground shopping center called **Forum des Halles.** The character of the neighborhood began to change, rents climbed, and many residents were forced to move away. Few of the original restaurants in the area remain today, and the neighborhood is currently undergoing a complete renovation.

You'll find several noteworthy examples of French architecture in this neighborhood. One is the beautiful and stately **Hôtel de Ville,** in the heart of the city. Another is the **Centre Pompidou.** When it opened in 1977, this center for contemporary art was criticized for its distinctive exterior, which features scaffolding and air ducts. Today, however, the building is an integral part of the cityscape. The area surrounding the Centre Pompidou is almost entirely closed to cars and is brimming with stores. If you're interested in checking out typical French retail chains, **Rue de Rivoli** is the perfect place.

Long ago, the Marais was a marshy area frequently under water. Starting in the 6th century, attempts had been made to drain the area but to little avail. A wall was built around it in the 12th century, which finally enabled the area to be drained, and the first building was erected around 1300. Later, the nobility built *hôtels particuliers* (grand residences) and eventually Paris's most beautiful square, **Place de Vosges,** was built. The Marais is a charming neighborhood with one-of-a-kind shops, hip restaurants, hidden courtyards, and narrow streets. The neighborhood is also well-known for its gay nightlife.

SHORT ON TIME? HERE ARE THE HIGHLIGHTS
+ LE CENTRE POMPIDOU + PLACE DES VOSGES + RUE DES ROSIERS
+ LE MARCHÉ DES ENFANTS ROUGES

TIPS
// Trendy gay neighborhood with a rich Jewish history
// Lots of great places to eat or get drinks
// Good for Sunday afternoon shopping

LES HALLES &
LE MARAIS

WALK 3 DESCRIPTION (approx. 4.1 miles)

Start the walk at Métro Étienne Marcel. Walk down Rue de Turbigo and turn right on Rue Montmartre ❶. There are nice shops on the second street on the left ❷. Continue straight on Rue de Montmartre ❸ and turn right on Rue L. Bellan ❹. Take a right on Rue Dussoubs. On the left you'll see the Passage du Grand Cerf—go in and check it out. Take a left on Rue de Tiquetonne for a nice men's clothing store ❺. Cross Rue de Turbigo to the right and turn left for a healthy snack ❻. Take a left on Rue Beaubourg for a nice lunch or dinner spot ❼. To continue, turn right and walk to Rue Rambuteau, then take another right. On the left is the Centre Pompidou ❽ ❾. Walk past the fountains toward Rue du Renard, then turn right and take this street to the Hôtel de Ville ❿. Then take Rue du Temple and turn right on Rue de la Verrerie ⓫. There is a recommended restaurant on the second street on the right ⓬. Continue on Rue de la Verrerie, then go left on Rue du Bourg Tibourg to explore a tea shop ⓭. At the end of the street, take a right. After passing a couple restaurants ⓮ ⓯, take a left and then an immediate right on Rue des Rosiers ⓰. The best pitas in Paris are down the first street on the right ⓱. Walk almost to the end of Rue des Rosiers ⓲ and turn right on Rue Pavée ⓳. Cross the busy street, and when you reach Métro St.-Paul, turn down Rue François Miron to find shops selling kids' things ⓴, or go left on Rue de Fourcy for a photo exhibit ㉑. Continue until you get to Rue Charlemagne, then turn left ㉒. At the end of the street take another left, then turn right on Rue St.-Antoine. Turn left on Rue de Birague toward Place des Vosges ㉓. Continue straight and take the second left for a bookshop and tea room ㉔. Turn left and then take the first street on the right ㉕ ㉖. For a Swedish lunch, take a right on Rue Payenne ㉗. Otherwise, continue straight until Rue Elzevir, where you can visit Musée Cognacq-Jay ㉘. After these detours, go back and continue the way you were going, past a wonderful restaurant ㉙ until Rue des Archives and turn right. Take the first right and then make a left on Rue Charlot for a name brand outlet ㉚, a covered market ㉛ and two trendy lunch spots ㉜ ㉝. Now take Rue de Normandie to the intersection with Rue de Turenne. Go diagonally to the left down Rue Froissart ㉞ ㉟. Turn right on Boulevard Beaumarchais for one of the nicest shops in Paris ㊱.

SIGHTS & ATTRACTIONS

① Due to a lack of funds, the construction of the **Église St.-Eustache** took more than a century—from 1532 to 1637. During this time styles changed, which is reflected in the mixture of Gothic and Renaissance styles. The basic structure is similar to that of Notre-Dame. The building has very tall ceilings, and the inside is lightly colored and ornately decorated. Famous figures including Richelieu, Molière, and Madame de Pompadour were baptized here. One surprising thing you'll find here is the triptych by contemporary artist Keith Haring.

2 impasse st.-eustache, www.saint-eustache.org, t: 0142363105, open mon-fri 9:30am-7pm, sat-sun 9am-7pm, free entrance, metro les halles

⑧ **Le Centre Pompidou**—called "Beaubourg" by the political left—was designed by architects Renzo Piano and Richard Rogers. The building was highly criticized when it opened in 1977, but quickly became an important Parisian landmark. The museum's permanent collection is comprised of more than 1,400 works of art. There are also numerous temporary exhibitions, as well as film screenings and conferences. Don't miss the bookshop, and be sure to go up to the top for a fantastic view out over the city.

place georges pompidou, www.centrepompidou.fr, t: 0144781233, open wed & fri-mon 11am-10pm, thu 11am-11pm, entrance €14, view only €3, metro rambuteau

⑩ For centuries, the **Hôtel de Ville de Paris** has been the center of political life in Paris. During the monarchy, the great square out front was the scene of public executions. In 1871 the Communards (supporters of the Paris Commune, the revolutionary government) set the building ablaze. Afterwards, it was fully restored according to its original design. In a hall on the side of the building there are often nice temporary exhibits, which you can access via the side entrance.

place de l'hôtel de ville, 4th arr., www.paris.fr, t: 0142764040, open tours by reservation, free entrance, metro hôtel de ville

⑲ The **Synagogue Agudath Hakehilot** was built in 1914 and designed by Art Nouveau architect Hector Guimard, who also designed the green cast-iron Métro

entrances. Germans blew up the synagogue during World War II, but it was later restored. Today it is a national monument.

10 rue pavée, 4th arr., t: 0148872154, not open to the public, metro st.-paul

㉑ The **MEP,** Maison Européenne de la Photographie, is located in a renovated hotel. The museum's collection includes works from big names such as Helmut Newton, Martin Parr, and Sarah Moon, but there is no permanent exhibition. The library on the ground floor is also worth a visit.

5-7 rue de fourcy, 4th arr., www.mep-fr.org, t: 0144787500, open wed-sun 11am-7:45pm, entrance €8, metro st.-paul/pont marie

㉖ **Musée Carnavalet** houses the history of the city, and is located in a typical Marais-style building with a beautiful adjoining garden. There are models of l'Île de la Cité and of the Bastille, along with maps, prints, and paintings—everything about life in Paris through the centuries. Unfortunately, the museum is closed until 2019.

16 rue des franc bourgeois, 3rd arr., www.carnavalet.paris.fr, t: 0144595858, open tue-sun 10am-6pm, free entrance permanent colletion (recommended donation €5), temporary exhibits €9, metro st.-paul/chemin vert

㉘ **Musée Cognacq-Jay** is a fairly unknown but wonderful museum. Here you can see the private collection of Ernest Cognacq and his wife Marie-Louise Jaÿ, which they collected between 1900 and 1925. This museum is recommended for anyone who loves paintings, drawings, porcelain, and furniture from the 18th century. The garden behind the museum holds a monument with a statue of George Washington, and a medallion representing Nicolas Martiau, his direct ancestor.

8 rue elzévir, 3rd arr., www.museecognacqjay.paris.fr, t: 0140270721, open tue-sun 10am-6pm, free entrance permanent collection, metro st.-paul/chemin vert

FOOD & DRINK

③ **Comptoir de la Gastronomie** began its *épicerie fine,* or gourmet store, at the end of the 19th century, selling traditional products such as foie gras and smoked fish. The restaurant serves regional French fare such as Burgundy-style escargots, duck confit, foie gras with honey, and crème brûlée. Each dish is paired with a delicious wine, which the staff will gladly advise you on.

34 rue montmartre, www.comptoirdelagastronomie.com, t: 0142333132, restaurant open mon-thu noon-11pm, fri-sat noon-midnight, store mon-sat 6am-8pm, price €20, metro les halles

④ Here you can enjoy delectable Corsican meals prepared with meat from Auvergne. The chef, who hails from Corsica, believes that this is the tastiest meat in France. The lunch and dinner menus at **Le Léopold** are updated every season. Locals come here to share a platter of charcuterie at the standing tables outside.

36 rue léopold bellan, 2nd arr., www.le-leopold.fr, t: 0145084583, open mon-fri noon-2:30pm & 6pm-10:30pm, sat 6pm-11pm, price €18, metro bourse/sentier

⑦ Restaurant **Le Derrière** is hidden away on a small square near two other nice places from the same owner: 404, a Moroccan restaurant, and Andy Whaloo, which serves good cocktails. At Le Derrière, they've done their best to create a unique dining environment. Each seating area is different, but they're all intended to make you feel at home. You can get a table in "the bedroom," where several of the seats are on an actual bed. Come here for the experience—the food itself is unexceptional. The Sunday brunch buffet, however, is recommended.

69 rue des gravilliers, 3rd arr., derriere-resto.com, t: 0144619195, open mon-sat noon-2:30pm & 8pm-11:30pm, sun noon-4:30pm & 8pm-11pm, price €30, sunday brunch €38, metro arts et metiers

⑨ Philippe Starck designed the modern decor at the trendy **Georges.** The restaurant is on the top floor of the Centre Pompidou and has a fantastic view out over the city, which is reflected in the price tag. The wait staff is a team of models—everything down to the very last detail here is beautiful.

place georges pompidou, www.beaumarly.com/en/restaurants/georges, t: 0144784799, open wed-mon noon-2am, price €38, metro rambuteau

⑫ From the outside, the bistro **Les Mauvais Garçons** stands out thanks to its green facade. The inside is understated with small tables, but the food is amazing

French fare influenced by southern cuisine from Lyon. Starters include dishes such as *camembert grillé* and *gratinée à l'oignon,* main courses such as *boeuf bourguignon* and *magret de canard,* and desserts such as *tarte à la praline rose.* Everything tastes just as delicious as it sounds!

4 rue des mauvais garçons, 4th arr., t: 0142727497, open wed-sun noon-2:30pm & 7pm-11:30pm, price €24, metro hôtel de ville

(14) There are countless reasons to have lunch or dinner at **Le Jaja.** The restaurant is in a sort of courtyard just beyond a busy street, and the trees and plants make it feel as if you are sitting in a secret garden. The Eastern-influenced menu is excellent and changes every season. To top it all off, they have an extensive wine list with some 80 wines. Locals come here for a glass of the best rosé.

3 rue ste.-croix de la bretonnerie, 4th arr., www.jaja-resto.com, t: 0142747152, open mon-sat noon-2:30pm & 7:30pm-11pm, sun noon-3pm & 7:30pm-10:30pm , price €23, metro hôtel de ville/st.-paul

(15) **Au Petit Fer à Cheval** in the Marais is a true classic. The café gets its name from its horseshoe-shaped bar made of zinc. Their outdoor seating is an ideal spot for people watching. The kitchen is open nonstop from noon to 1:15am— a real rarity in Paris. So come here any day for a late lunch.

30 rue vieille du temple, 4th arr., www.cafeine.com, t: 0142724747, open daily 9am-1:15am, price €15, metro hôtel de ville/st.-paul

(17) At **Miznon** you can get the best pitas in town. "Miznon" is Hebrew for "buffet." Order at the bar, selecting from the ingredients written on the chalkboard, then watch them being stuffed into your pocket bread. There is plenty to choose from. Try the mouth-watering lamb kebab, *boeuf bourguignon,* carrot ratatouille, or fresh marinated tuna. Prefer something sweet? Try a banana-chocolate pita. You can sit and eat at the bar or at the tables in the dining area.

22 rue des écouffes, 4th arr., t: 0142748358, open mon-thu & sun noon-11:30pm, fri noon-4pm, price €13, metro st.-paul

(18) You could easily spend the entire afternoon at tea room **Le Loir dans la Théière.** Sink into one of the comfortable armchairs and enjoy a pot of tea and

an indescribably delicious *tarte au citron-meringuée,* or a generous slice of any of the other many freshly baked tarts.

3 rue des rosiers, 4th arr., t: 0142729061, open daily 9:30am-7:30pm, price lunch €18, metro st.-paul

㉗ **Le Café Suédois** is a nice spot for a simple Swedish lunch. The courtyard is particularly pleasant, but there are also tables inside. On the menu you'll find things such as Swedish salmon, meatballs, and cinnamon buns.

11 rue payenne, 3rd arr., paris.si.se, t: 0144788011, open tue-sun noon-6pm, price €8, metro st.-paul/chemin vert

㉙ **Le Dôme du Marais** is a nice restaurant in the middle of the Marais. It has a covered terrace where you can stop in the afternoon for a cup of tea and something sweet. Inside is a circular dining area. This is a great spot for brunch, lunch or dinner. As the name suggests, the restaurant's ceiling is a large, round glass dome. Be sure to reserve a table in advance.

53 bis rue des francs bourgeois, 4th arr., www.ledomedumarais.fr, t: 0142745417, open daily restaurant noon-2:30pm & 7pm-11pm, tea room 2:30pm-7pm, price main course €30, sunday brunch €30, metro hôtel de ville/rambuteau/st.-paul

㉜ Try a bento box—a Japanese lunch box meal—at **Nanashi.** Nanashi is a Japanese chain with three restaurants in Paris. The bentos include healthy fare such as rice, salad, salmon and fresh vegetables. Order one of their fresh juices to go with your meal, such as the carrot ginger juice. Nanashi is a popular spot among Paris's models.

57 rue charlot, 3rd arr., www.nanashi.fr, t: 0960002559, open mon-fri noon-3pm & 7:30pm-11pm, sat-sun noon-4pm & 7:30pm-11pm, price €13, metro filles du calvaire

㉝ **Café Pinson** is super trendy and 100% healthy. The San Francisco-inspired decor is light and airy, with lots of comfy places to sit. You immediately feel at home here. Order a fresh juice and a detox meal, like a healthy salad with seeds or risotto with veggies and spices. It is always busy here, so come early to avoid a long line or get your food to go.

6 rue du forez, www.cafepinson.fr, t: 0983825353, open mon-fri 9am-midnight, sat 10am-midnight, sun noon-6pm, price €13, metro filles du calvaire

㉞ Stop by **Le Mary Céleste** for a break at the big wooden bar in front of the large open windows. Share a plate of oysters during oyster season (from September to April). Or choose a dish from the menu, which changes daily, and end the night with a cocktail.

1 rue commines, 3rd arr., www.lemaryceleste.com, t: 0980729883, open daily 6pm-11:30pm, price cocktail €12, oysters €2-5 each, metro filles de calvaire

SHOPPING

② When you walk in the store at **Baobab,** you're met with a riot of colors. Here you'll find all kinds of household items: pillows, pillowcases, bags, dishes, lampshades, etc. There are also racks of clothes in all colors of the rainbow.

2 rue du jour, 1st arr., www.baobab-home.fr, t: 0984157947, open mon 2:30pm-7:30pm, tue-sat 10:30am-7:30pm, metro st.-etienne/les halles

⑤ In this section of the Rue Tiquetonne you'll find plenty of nice men's clothing stores. The small shop **Royal Cheese** has shoes, hats, and jeans from different brands, including Selvedge, Edwin, and Woolrich.

22-24 rue tiquetonne, 2nd arr., www.royalcheese.com, t: 0142213065, open mon-sat 11am-8pm, metro réaumur sebastopol/étienne marcel

⑥ **L'Amoncel** is a good spot to stop for a healthy snack. The shop sells a variety of nuts in an assortment of flavors. Since its inception in 2013 the concept has quickly caught on and the store is now known for its quality products. All nuts are roasted and/or salted on site. Don't miss their dried fruits and delicious chocolate barks.

1 rue étienne marcel, 1st arr., www.lamoncel.com, t: 0140130652, open mon-sat 10am-8:30pm, metro étienne marcel

⑪ **BHV** (Bazar de l'Hôtel de Ville), a department store spread across seven stories and multiple buildings, sells everything. The basement, for example, is a paradise for *bricoleurs*, with a hardware department that would amaze any DIYer. It also has a nice, big toy department. BHV organizes events and activities, such as live DJs at its restaurant Cour Bleu and the rooftop bar Le

Perchoir Marais during the summer months. Check out the website for the latest events.

52 rue de rivoli, www.bhv.fr, t: 0142749000, open mon-sat 9:30am-8pm, sun 11am-7pm, metro hôtel de ville

⑬ **Mariage Frères** is the perfect spot to sip tea and eat cake. The store is also worth a visit. Peruse the list of over 100 types of teas and ask to smell one or two. In addition to tea, they sell beautiful cups and teapots for tea ceremonies. This chain has been around since 1854 and has locations throughout Paris and the world.

30 rue du bourg-tibourg, www.mariagefreres.com, t: 0142722811, store open 10:30am-7:30pm, restaurant noon-3pm, tea room 3pm-7pm, metro st.-paul/hôtel de ville

⑳ Color is everywhere at **Petit Pan.** The unique collections of kids' clothing and objects are sure to lighten your heart. The delicate lanterns are especially beautiful, and the dozens of jars filled with buttons and other doodads are fun.

37, 39 & 76 rue françois miron, 4th arr., www.petitpan.com, t: 0144549084, open tue-sat 10:30am-7:30pm, metro st.-paul

㉔ The concept at **Le Salon by Thé des Écrivains** is a winner: A bookstore with a tucked-away tea room. Choose from nine types of tea, and don't forget the delicious cake too. This is the ideal spot for an indulgent break. Grab a book, sit back and relax a while. The venue also organizes lots of debates, book presentations and documentary screenings. It's a good spot for lunch, or even Sunday brunch (by reservation only).

16 rue des minimes, 3rd arr., www.thedesecrivains.com, t: 0140294625, open tue-sun 11:30am-7:30pm, price tea and cake €10, metro st.-paul

㉕ Nearly all French people, young and old alike, have a pair of Bensimon sneakers in their closet. The beloved concept store **Home Autour du Monde** sells them in all styles and sizes. In addition, the store carries the Bensimon clothing line—not to mention a great selection of furniture, home goods, and nice gift ideas.

8 rue des francs bourgeois, 3rd arr., www.bensimon.com, t: 0142770608, open mon 11am-7pm, tue-sat 10:30am-7pm, sun 11am-7pm, metro st.-paul

③⓪ L'Habilleur sells clothes from the previous season at up to 50% off. You can find clothes here from designers such as Olivier Strelli, Martine Sitbon, Patrick Cox, Dice Kayek and other top name brands.

44 rue de poitou, 3rd arr., www.lhabilleur.fr, t: 0148877712, open mon-sat noon-7:30pm, metro st.-sébastien froissart

③⑤ Bonton is a true paradise for kids: three floors of Bonton brand clothing, accessories, knickknacks, furniture, bed linens, and anything else you could wish for. There is even a children's hair stylist.

5 boulevard des filles du calvaire, 3rd arr., www.bonton.fr, t: 0142723469, open mon-sat 10am-7pm, metro filles du calvaire

③⑥ Merci is a concept store with a do-good dimension—a portion of profits go to a foundation that helps fund school meals for kids in Madagascar. The mini department store has a unique, thoughtful collection of clothing, decorations, kitchen items and furniture. The underlying theme here is hip and sustainable. In the basement, La Cantine Merci is a popular lunch spot. On the ground floor is the Used Book Café, and one door down is the Merci Cinema Café. Further on down the street, at number 91, is their pizzeria Grazie.

111 boulevard beaumarchais, www.merci-merci.com, t: 0142770033, open mon-sat 10am-7pm, metro st.-sebastien froissart

MORE TO EXPLORE

⑯ The **Rue des Rosiers** is a great street for traditional Jewish food and falafel. If you want to sit down, try to snag a table at Chez Marianne on the corner of Rue des Hospitalières-St.-Gervais.

rue des rosiers, 4th arr., open daily noon-11pm, metro st.-paul

㉒ **Le Village St.-Paul** was established when the neighborhood underwent a period of restoration and renovation. It is a labyrinth of courtyards, galleries, bookshops, antique stores, restaurants and cafés. Just walking through this secluded, cozy area is a pleasure of its own.

le village st.-paul, between quai des celestins, rue st.-paul and rue charlemagne, 4th arr., www.levillagesaintpaul.com, open daily 11am-7pm, metro st.-paul/pont marie

㉓ **Place des Vosges** is thought by many to be the most beautiful square in Paris. The Marais was once a community favored by the aristocracy and wealthy bourgeoisie, and in 1605 King Henry IV had the wonderful idea of making a park here enclosed by 36 houses. Many famous French people have lived here, including Cardinal Richelieu at number 21 and author Victor Hugo at number 6. This is a great spot for a break—either on a bench or on one of the terraces.

place des vosges, 4th arr., metro st.-paul/bastille

㉛ **Le Marché des Enfants Rouges** is the oldest market in Paris. It gets its names from an orphanage that used to be nearby where the children were always dressed in red clothing. The covered market, which is open most days, has a couple dozen stalls where you can buy a variety of fresh products. The market also has a lot of spots to eat, and Parisians from across the city flock here for breakfast, lunch and dinner.

39 rue de bretagne, open tue-sat 8am-8:30pm, sun 8am-5pm, metro filles du calvaire

WALK **4**

NOTRE-DAME, QUARTIER LATIN & ST.-GERMAIN-DES-PRES

ABOUT THE WALK

This walk takes you over across the Seine to Paris's Left Bank, primarily through the 5th and 6th arrondissements. Consider splitting the walk over two days so you have extra time to stop and enjoy the scenic parks you come to along the way. The 5th arrondissement (locations 1-23) is especially interesting during the day, and the 6th is great in the early evening when you can relax and enjoy a nice drink and dinner (locations 24-34).

THE NEIGHBORHOODS

In the heart of the city, smack dab in the middle of the Seine, lie the islands **Île de la Cité** and **Île St.-Louis.** On the former stands the spectacular **Notre-Dame,** its towers peeking out above the skyline. You'll find an inconspicuous bronze compass rose labeled **Point Zéro** on the square in front of the cathedral. Since 1769, the distance of all roads to and from Paris have been measured in reference to this spot. It is no coincidence that it's located on Île de la Cité—this island is where Paris began.

For centuries the Left Bank of the Seine, or **Rive Gauche,** has had great cultural significance. After the arrival of the **university** in 1215 and then later a printing press, it became the intellectual and literary heart of the city. Scholars, writers, and publishers settled here, along with countless bookshops and writers' cafés. Later, the arrival of artists brought galleries as well. The Quartier Latin, or Latin Quarter—Paris's student area—is located around the Ste.-Geneviève hill. **Rue Mouffetard** is one of the oldest streets in Paris, with lots of restaurants and bars.

The St.-Germain-des-Près neighborhood became an intellectual and literary center in its own right. In local nightclubs, philosophy, politics, and literature were discussed against backdrops of smoke and jazz music. Sartre, De Beauvoir,

Hemingway, and Capote were all regulars at **Café de Flore.** The vivid atmosphere of yesteryear is still palpable here today.

There are two green oases in the 5th and 6th arrondissements: **Le Jardin des Plantes,** which features a botanic garden, and **Le Jardin du Luxembourg,** where the **Palais du Luxembourg** is located. Originally built for Marie de Médici, today the palace houses the French Senate.

SHORT ON TIME? HERE ARE THE HIGHLIGHTS
+ NOTRE-DAME DE PARIS + LE JARDIN DU LUXEMBOURG
+ LA MOSQUÉE DE PARIS + CAFÉ DE FLORE + RUE MOUFFETARD

TIPS
// Must-do route for first-time visitors
// Walk through the most beautiful parks of Paris
// Suitable for biking

NOTRE-DAME, QUARTIER LATIN & ST.-GERMAIN-DES-PRES

WALK 4 DESCRIPTION (approx. 7.2 miles)

Start the walk at Métro Pont Neuf, then cross the bridge to the two buildings on the left halfway across. Turn on Rue H. Robert toward Place Dauphine ❶. Walk on the left over Quai de l'Horloge until Boulevard du Palais, where you take a right ❷ ❸. You are now on Île de la Cité ❹. Cross the Pont St.-Michel bridge and take an immediate left. Turn right at the next bridge on Rue du Petit Pont for some Parisian entertainment ❺. Take Rue St.-Julien and the Pont au Double bridge to Notre-Dame ❻. Walk behind the cathedral to Île St.-Louis for the best ice cream in Paris ❼. Take Pont de la Tournelle back over to the Left Bank. Take a left for the Institut du Monde Arabe ❽. Head back to Quai de la Tournelle and turn left on Rue Pontoise ❾. At the end of the street, go a short way to the right to reach Rue Monge. Take this street, with a little detour into the candy shop ❿, and continue until the arena ⓫. Go through the arena and down Rue des Arènes. Cross Rue Linné toward Rue G. de la Bosse and, at the end of the street, make a right and head towards the Jardin des Plantes ⓬. Exit the park at Rue Geoffroy, where you'll find a beautiful museum ⓭. Cross the street ⓮ and continue straight on Rue Daubenton ⓯. Cross Rue Monge to continue on Rue Daubenton until Rue Mouffetard ⓰ ⓱. Here you'll find a variety of shops and cafés ⓲. Walk down Rue Mouffetard until you come to Place de la Contrescarpe ⓳. Turn left here on Rue Thouin toward the Panthéon ⓴. Go left on Rue Soufflot for cocktails ㉑ or take a right to catch a movie ㉒ and visit a museum ㉓. Walk back in the direction you came from and turn right toward Boulevard St.-Michel. Make a left and head toward the park ㉔. Walk through the park and take the exit left of the Senate, coming out at Rue Férou, and follow that to St.-Sulpice. There is a lot of good shopping on Rue du Vieux Colombier ㉕ ㉖. Go back to Rue St.-Sulpice and, at the end, make a left and go past Métro Odéon. On Boulevard St.-Germain turn right and walk a short distance, then go left on Rue St.-André des Arts ㉗. Walk to the end of the street, then continue down Rue Buci on the left toward Rue de Seine ㉘. Take Rue de l'Abbaye to Place Furstenberg ㉙ and continue on to Place St.-Germain-des-Prés for some cafés ㉚. Take Rue de Rennes to Rue B. Palissy ㉛, and then take Rue du Dragon toward Place M. Debré. Turn right on Rue de Grenelle for shoes ㉜ or left for clothes ㉝. Then head down Rue de Sèvres to Rue Dupin, where you can turn left to end the day ㉞.

SIGHTS & ATTRACTIONS

② **La Conciergerie** was Paris's first prison. The revolutionary Georges Danton was one of the many who did time here, along with Marie-Antoinette and Robespierre. Marie-Antoinette's cell has been made into a commemorative chapel you can visit.

2 boulevard du palais, 1st arr., www.paris-conciergerie.fr, t: 0153406080, open daily 9:30am-6pm, entrance €8.50, metro cité

③ **Sainte-Chapelle** was built in the time of St. Louis, King of France, to house Christ's crown of thorns and a relic of the Holy Cross. The cathedral has two chapels: a lower one for the king's servants, and an upper one for the royal family. The beautiful stained-glass windows are unique and have significant cultural and historical value.

8 boulevard du palais, 1st arr., www.sainte-chapelle.fr, t: 0153406080, open daily: march-oct 9:30am-6pm, nov-feb 9am-5pm, entrance €8.50, metro cité

⑥ The interior of the impressive Gothic cathedral **Notre-Dame de Paris** is richly decorated with stained-glass windows and countless statues. It also houses one of the largest organs in the world. Napoleon was crowned emperor in this cathedral. Although it can be very busy here, it is entirely worth the visit. Through a side entrance you can climb the stairs to the top of the tower, where you'll be rewarded with a fantastic view of the city.

6 parvis notre-dame, 4th arr., www.notredamedeparis.fr, open cathedral mon-fri 8am-6:45pm, sat-sun 8am-7:15pm, towers 10am-5:30pm, free entrance to cathedral, towers €8.50, metro cité/st.-michel

⑧ The building that houses the **Institut du Monde Arabe** was designed in the 1980s by Jean Nouvel. The exterior is covered in thousands of small steel mobile apertures, which gradually open and close based on the amount of sunshine. Inside you'll find an impressive collection of Arabic design, including contemporary art, calligraphy and musical instruments. Head up to the roof terrace and enjoy the view over the Seine and Notre-Dame.

1 rue des fossés st.-bernard, 5th arr., www.imarabe.org, t: 0142345610, open tue-thu 10am-6pm, fri 10am-9:30pm, sat-sun 10am-7pm, entrance €8, metro jussieu

OMMES · LA · PATRIE · R

⑪ The **Arènes de Lutèce** is considered to be the oldest building in Paris. Seating in the amphitheater accommodated approximately 17,000 spectators, who could enter through 41 different entrances.

47 rue monge, 5th arr., open daily: summer 9am-9:30pm, winter 8am-7:30pm, free entrance, metro cardinal lemoine

⑬ In **Musée National d'Histoire Naturelle**'s Grande Galerie de l'Évolution you can learn all about evolution and the relationship between nature and the human race. This beautifully renovated glass and metal space contains an unprecedented collection of taxidermy animals.

36 rue geoffroy-st.-hilaire, 5th arr., www.mnhn.fr, t: 0140513838, open wed-mon 10am-6pm, entrance €10, metro censier-daubenton/austerlitz/jussieu

⑳ **Le Panthéon** is one of architect Soufflot's greatest works. Following the French Revolution, this former church was transformed into a crypt where more than 70 famous French figures are interred, including Voltaire, Rousseau, Hugo, and Zola.

place du panthéon, 5th arr., pantheon.monuments-nationaux.fr, t: 0144321800, open daily: april-sept 10am-6:30pm, oct-march 10am-6pm, entrance €7.50, metro cardinal lemoine

㉓ **Musée de Cluny** is dedicated to the Middle Ages. Many stories from this time are reflected in the series of tapestries entitled *The Lady and the Unicorn*— a perfect example of the *mille-fleurs* style. Don't forget to check out the Gallo-Roman baths, too.

6 place paul painlevé, 5th arr., www.musee-moyenage.fr, t: 0153737816, open wed-mon 9:15am-5:45pm, entrance €8, metro cluny-la sorbonne/st.-michel/odéon

㉙ **Musée National Eugène Delacroix** is located in the painter's former house. The artist's studio paints a good picture not only of Delacroix himself, but also of the artistic movement he was a part of: Romanticism. Be sure to also walk back to Place de Furstenberg, a beautiful hidden square.

6 rue de furstenberg, 6th arr., www.musee-delacroix.fr, t: 0144418650, open wed-mon 9:30am-5:30pm, entrance €7, metro st.-germain-des-prés/mabillon

FOOD & DRINK

⑤ **Aux Trois Mailletz**—you either love it or you hate it. This isn't the place for an outstanding meal, but rather for the atmosphere and entertainment. Enjoy a drink and piano music upstairs, or head into the basement for music, dance and a show. Among Parisians, Trois Mailletz has long been known as a place to go for a fun—albeit unpredictable—evening.

56 rue galande, 5th arr., www.lestroismailletz.fr, t: 0143540079, open daily: piano bar from 6pm, cabaret 8:30pm-5am, restaurant 7pm-5am, price €25, metro cité/st.-michel

⑦ Ice cream in France isn't nearly as popular as gelato in Italy. However, **Berthillon** is an exception to the rule. This shop has irresistibly delicious sorbets and hands down the best ice cream in Paris. You'll want to stand in line for that!

31 rue st.-louis en l'ile, 4th arr., www.berthillon.fr, t: 0143543161, open wed-sun 10am-8pm, metro pont marie

⑯ The clientele at **Le Mouffetard** is as diverse as the neighborhood and includes marketgoers, shop employees, students, and tourists. Here, everyone feels at home. It is a true *bar de quartier* (neighborhood bar), and is the best place to sit and take in what's happening on Rue Mouffetard.

116 rue mouffetard, 5th arr., t: 0143314250, open tue-sun 7:30am-7pm, price €15, metro cardinal lemoine

⑲ Ernest Hemingway once described **Café Delmas**'s predecessor—Café des Amateurs—as "the cesspool of the Rue Mouffetard." The current Café Delmas is enormously popular among local high school students. The terrace is nice and spacious, and is the perfect place to soak up the neighborhood vibe.

2 place de la contrescarpe, 5th arr., www.cafedelmasparis.com, t: 0143265126, open daily 7:30am-2am, price €18, metro cardinal lemoine

㉑ For anyone who has ever been a student in Paris, **Le Crocodile** is something of an institution. The small, dark cocktail bar has a rich history, and for years the concept has remained unchanged. Inside you're shown to a small spot on a bench, where you can choose from among the 365 different cocktails on the menu. At the bottom of your glass you'll find a nice surprise—a little crocodile

candy. The vibe at Le Crocodile is open and friendly, and before you know it you'll be spending the entire night chatting with everyone around you.

6 rue royer-collard, 5th arr., t: 0143543237, open mon-sat 6pm-2am, price cocktail €12, metro place monge

(27) Somewhat hidden away, on the nicest street in the neighborhood, you'll find **La Jacobine.** This is a great place to come for a nice lunch, afternoon tea, heavenly pastries or dinner. The atmosphere is warm and inviting, and the dishes seem as if they've come straight out of grandma's kitchen. La Jacobine is increasingly popular and, especially in the evenings, you can expect a wait for a table.

59 rue st.-andré des arts, 6th arr., t: 0146341595, open tue-sun noon-11pm, mon 7pm-11pm, price €18, metro odéon

(28) The terrace at **Le Bar du Marché** is an ideal spot for people watching. The café is on the corner of Rue de Buci, which is a nice, busy market street. The friendly servers—with their blue overalls and newsboy caps—will remind you of street kids from another time.

75 rue de seine, 6th arr., t: 0143265515, open daily 8am-2am, price €15, metro mabillon/odéon

(30) You can't say that you've truly experienced St.-Germain-des-Prés until you've had a coffee at **Café de Flore.** You can almost taste the café's history. Existentialists such as Jean-Paul Sartre and Simone de Beauvoir were regulars here, as were Pablo Picasso and writer André Breton.

172 boulevard st.-germain, 6th arr., www.cafedeflore.fr, t: 0145485526, open daily 7am-2am, price lunch €18, metro st.-germain-des-prés

(31) **Eggs & Co**. is only open during the day, which makes it an ideal place for brunch or lunch. As the name suggests, this restaurant is all about eggs, served up in a variety of ways: with salmon, on an English muffin, in a salad, hard boiled, fried—take your pick.

11 rue bernard palissy, 6th arr., www.eggsandco.fr, t: 0145440252, open daily 10am-6pm, price €15, metro st.-germain-des-prés

㉞ In this French bistro you'll find locals and tourists alike. **L'Epi Dupin** is a nice place to go with friends to enjoy a good meal. The food is beautifully presented and the menu changes regularly. Considering the quality, the prices are also quite reasonable. This restaurant is popular, so it's best to reserve a table in advance.

11 rue dupin, 6th arr., www.epidupin.com, t: 0142226456, open tue-fri noon-3pm & 7pm-11pm, mon 7pm-11pm, price €28, metro sèvres babylone

SHOPPING

⑩ **Le Bonbon au Palais** is a wonderful shop with glass candy dishes full of sweets from all across France. The enthusiastic owner will happily tell you about each candy, including where it comes from and what makes it so special. Who knows, he might even let you sample something, such as the candied violets made with all-natural ingredients.

19 rue monge, 5th arr., www.bonbonsaupalais.fr, t: 0178561572, open tue-sat 10:30am-7:30pm, metro cardinal lemoine

⑮ The owners of **Maison Franco-Orientale** describe their shop as being similar to a *souk* (an Arabic market) or like Ali Baba's cave. Here you'll find all types of Eastern objects, such as Afghan jewelry and tea cups. They also have an enormous collection of North African shoes called *babouches*.

19 rue daubenton, 5th arr., t: 0147070757, open daily 10:30am-8pm, metro place monge/censier-daubenton

⑱ It is always fun to look around at **L'Epée de Bois.** First, because owners Rémi and Geneviève are so friendly. Second, because the store is a colorful world full of fantasy and fun for kids aged 0-12. The handmade toys here are beautiful.

12 rue de l'épée de bois, 5th arr., t: 0143315018, open mon 1:30pm-7:30pm, tue-sat 10:30am-7:30pm, sun 11am-1:30pm, metro place monge/censier-daubenton

㉕ Within the French world of fashion, **Agnès b** is something of a household name. Pieces from the brand's comfortable and stylish collection are the basics in any Parisian fashionista's wardrobe—be it woman or man. The Agnès b

femme and homme lines are presented in a decor that perfectly complements the clothing.

6 rue du vieux colombier, 6th arr., t: 0144390260, open summer: mon-sat 10:30am-7:30pm, winter: mon-sat 10am-7pm, metro st.-sulpice

㉖ **Zadig & Voltaire** began in 1996 with one small shop in the Marais. Today, the brand has stores around the world. In Paris, the ready-to-wear label has developed something of a cult following among the city's young and not-so-young alike. The brand's fine cashmere sweaters come in a variety of colors and continue to be some of its best sellers.

1-3 rue du vieux colombier, 6th arr., www.zadig-et-voltaire.com, t: 0145483937, open mon-sat 10:30am-7:30pm, metro st.-sulpice

㉜ In the chic shopping street Rue de Grenelle, **Iris** is a place worth checking out. In this unpretentious store you'll find shoes from a variety of top designers, including Marc Jacobs, Chloé, Viktor&Rolf, and Veronique Branquinho.

28 rue de grenelle, 7th arr., www.irisshoes.com, t: 0142228981, open mon-sat 11am-7pm, metro st.-sulpice/rue du bac

㉝ There are some 25 **Claudie Pierlot** boutiques across Paris. Here you'll find nice, unique clothing at a range of prices. The clothes are hip and stylish, and come in mostly basic colors such as black and white—there is sure to be something for everyone. This is a great place to stop in and browse.

23 rue du vieux colombier, 6th arr., www.claudiepierlot.com, t: 0145481196, open mon-sat 10:30am-7:30pm, metro st.-sulpice

MORE TO EXPLORE

① **Place Dauphine,** located behind the Palais de Justice, is a pleasant and unexpected place to sit and take a break. The stately buildings surrounding the square block out the noise of the city and, in the summer, the trees provide full shade. There are plenty of benches where you can relax and read a book or observe a game of *pétanque.*

place dauphine, l'Île de la cité, 1st arr., metro pont neuf

④ **Île de la Cité** is the island around which Paris developed. It was originally two uninhabited islands, Île aux Vaches ("island of cows") and Île Notre-Dame, which belonged to the cathedral. In the early 17th century, the two islands were joined by Christophe Marie, and by around 1664 they were completely built up.

4th arr., metro cité

⑨ The **Piscine Pontoise** was built in 1934 by Lucien Pollet, who designed four such swimming pools in France. The pool has been listed as a historical building since 1981. The blue changing rooms on the mezzanine give a unique and interesting look to the Art Deco pool. On certain days the pool is open for nighttime swimming.

19 rue de pontoise, 5th arr., equipement.paris.fr/piscine-pontoise-2918, t: 0155427788, open mon-fri 7am-8:30am, 12:15pm-1:30pm, 4:30pm-7pm, 8:15pm-11:45pm, sat 10am-7pm, sun 8am-7pm, entrance day €4.80, night €11.10, metro maubert mutualité

⑫ The beautiful **Jardin des Plantes** is a must-see for all garden lovers. You can walk through the botanic gardens and the rose gardens, and visit the giant greenhouses. There is even a zoo and a playground here.

57 rue cuvier, 5th arr., www.jardindesplantes.net, t: 0140795601, garden open daily: summer 7:30am-8pm, winter 8am-5:30pm, greenhouses wed-mon: summer 10am-6pm, winter 10am-5pm, price garden free entrance, greenhouses €6, metro censier-daubenton/austerlitz

⑭ **La Mosquée de Paris** was built in 1922 as a monument to Muslim victims of the First World War. The mosque is open to the public, but don't forget to take your shoes off when you enter. Here you can treat your body and soul at the *hammam* and in the prayer hall. There is also an excellent tea room here where you can enjoy mint tea and a large assortment of sweets and other yummy snacks. For a full meal, try the restaurant.

39 rue st.-hilaire, 5th arr., www.la-mosquee.com, t: 0143311432, open daily 9am-noon & 2pm-6pm, restaurant 12:30pm-3pm & 7:30pm-midnight, tea room 9am-midnight, hammam for women only wed-mon 10am-9pm, metro place monge

⑰ One of Paris's oldest streets, **Rue Mouffetard** dates back to the time of Roman domination. During the Middle Ages, many craftsmen had their shops here because of the proximity to the Bièvre River. Be sure to pay attention to all of the ornamentation on the building facades, such as the painting at number 134. The famous morning market nearby, at Église St.-Médard, has been around since the seventh century. Local producers sell their products here—from fresh fruits and vegetables to homemade cheeses. The many restaurants and cafés on the street also make a stroll here well worth your while.

rue mouffetard, 5th arr., market open wed, fri & sun 8am-2pm, metro place monge

㉒ **Cinéma du Panthéon** is one of the oldest movie theaters in Paris. Come here not just to catch a movie, but also for a drink or bite to eat at Le Salon, which was decorated by the French actress Catherine Deneuve. Note: Le Salon is only open during the week.

13 rue victor cousin, 5th arr., www.whynotproductions.fr, t: 0140460121, movie theater: see website for times and prices, salon open: mon-fri noon-7pm, metro luxembourg/cluny-la sorbonne

㉔ **Le Jardin du Luxembourg** is a wonderful park where Parisians love to come to relax, have fun and walk around. The park is dotted throughout with the iconic "Luxembourg chairs." Also located here is the Palais de Luxembourg, which was built between 1615 and 1627 for Marie de Médici and today houses the French Senate.

rue de vaurigard/boulevard st.-michel, 6th arr., www.senat.fr/visite/jardin, t: 0142342362, open from sunrise to sunset, free entrance, rer luxembourg/metro odéon

WALK **5**

EIFFEL TOWER, INVALIDES & CHAMPS-ELYSEES

ABOUT THE WALK

This long walk is best to do when the weather is nice. You can follow this route in either direction. The section of the walk from the Eiffel Tower over Les Berges de la Seine and up to Rue de Bac can be done by bike. You can also cycle over the Champs-Élysées from the Concorde to the Arc de Triomphe—it's a decent stretch—but be sure to get off your bike before the Arc de Triomphe roundabout. If you'd rather not walk the Champs-Élysées, hop on Métro line 1.

THE NEIGHBORHOODS

Paris is full of grand, historical buildings. The city can thank Louis XIV for its classic character and Renaissance influence. He had Les Invalides built in the 17th century for his wounded officers and soldiers. Later Napoleon introduced the style Napoleon—or Empire style—in Paris, based on ancient Egyptian and Roman architecture. Napoleon had the **Arc de Triomphe** built in this style. Paris's classic wide boulevards and avenues were built between 1852 and 1870 during the Second French Empire under the rule of Napoleon III.

Avenue des Champs-Élysées connects Place Charles de Gaulle, where the **Arc de Triomphe** stands, with **Place de la Concorde.** The avenue dates back to the 17th century, when it was just a long road in an area with nothing much going on. In 1828, the city laid its first pavements here. Today, the Champs-Élysées is renowned as a shopping mecca, with all of the best-known retail chains and long opening hours. There are also several big movie theaters on this boulevard.

In the late 19th century, French architects began to incorporate materials such as iron and glass into their work. This new style is reflected in the **Eiffel Tower, Le Grand Palais, Le Petit Palais,** and **Pont Alexandre III,** which were built for the World's Fairs.

In recent years, city officials have taken initiatives to make Paris more livable for residents. **Les Berges de la Seine** was born out of one of these initiatives. In 2013, the road on the Left Bank of the Seine between the Eiffel Tower and the **Musée d'Orsay** was turned into a recreational area. Every summer this area is further extended thanks to Paris Plages (temporary beaches along the Seine), and cars have to cede another part of the waterfront road to pedestrians, cyclists, and skaters.

SHORT ON TIME? HERE ARE THE HIGHLIGHTS
**+ EIFFEL TOWER + PALAIS DE TOKYO + MUSÉE RODIN
+ MUSÉE D'ORSAY + CHAMPS-ELYSEES**

TIPS

// Must-do route for first-time visitors
// Certain parts are suitable for biking
// Stroll past some of the most notable sights

SIGHTS & ATTRACTIONS

① The exhibitions in the experimental 21st-century **Palais de Tokyo** are always unique and boundary-pushing, with light and sound effects and moving objects. The space is enormous, so it can contain large objects. The exhibits vary tremendously, but there is always something to discover. The museum shop is also worth a visit—it sells unique books and fun knickknacks. The restaurant with outdoor seating serves international fare.

13 avenue du président wilson, 16th arr., www.palaisdetokyo.com, t: 018973588, open wed-mon noon-midnight, entrance €10, metro iéna

② The building containing the Palais de Tokyo, built for the 1937 World's Fair, also houses the **Musée d'Art Moderne.** In this museum of modern art you'll find an extensive collection of 20th- and 21st-century art owned by the city of Paris.

11 avenue du président wilson, 16th arr., www.mam.paris.fr, t: 0153674000, open tue-wed & fri-sun 10am-6pm, thu 10am-10pm, free entrance to permanent collection, metro iéna / alma-marceau

④ The neoclassical **Palais de Chaillot,** designed by four architects, was also built for the 1937 World's Fair. Today it houses La Cité de l'Architecture et du Patrimoine museum. Even if you're not interested in visiting the museum, take a look inside. Out back you'll find a terrace with an amazing view of the Eiffel Tower.

1 place du trocadéro, 16th arr., www.citechaillot.fr, t: 01158515200, open fri-mon & wed 11am-7pm, thu 11am-9pm, entrance €8, metro trocadéro

⑤ The **Eiffel Tower** (La Tour Eiffel), another World's Fair monument, was built in 1889. Initially Gustave Eiffel's design was met with great resistance, but the Eiffel Tower has since become the symbol of Paris. From the third balcony you can see as far as 65 kilometers (40 miles) away. The line to visit the Tower often seems endless—sometimes it helps to go either very early or very late. Tip: Buy your ticket online beforehand.

champs de mars, 7th arr., www.toureiffel.paris, t: 0892701239, open daily 9:30am-11pm, mid june-end aug 9am-midnight, entrance €5-15.50, metro bir-hakeim

⑥ The **Musée du Quai Branly,** which opened in 2006, is located in a striking building. This museum of *les arts lointains* exhibits approximately 3,500 works of indigenous art from places like Africa and Oceania. The building is surrounded by a beautiful park with a *mur végétal* (wall of plants) on the Seine side.
37 quai branly, 7th arr., www.quaibranly.fr, t: 0156617000, open tue-wed & sun 11am-7pm, thu-sat 11am-9pm, entrance €9, metro iéna / alma-marceau / rer pont de l'alma

⑩ The **Pont Alexandre III** is the most elegant bridge in Paris, in part because of its beautiful golden statues. It was built over two years for the 1900 World's Fair.
pont alexandre III, 8th arr., metro champs-élysées clemenceau / invalides

⑫ In 1670, Louis XIV had **Les Invalides** built as a resting place for soldiers wounded during his numerous wars. Napoleon was laid to rest here in 1861 in the crypt under the golden dome. The building also houses the Musée de l'Armée, which is dedicated to French military history. Whenever a new French president is inaugurated, the cannons in front of Les Invalides fire 21 times.
129 rue de grenelle, 7th arr., www.musee-armee.fr, t: 0144423877, open daily april-oct 10am-6pm, nov-march 10am-5pm, entrance €9.50, courtyard free, metro invalides

⑬ **Musée Rodin** is located in the sculptor's former residence. In addition to Rodin's own sculptures and studies, the museum also exhibits the work of Camille Claudel, Rodin's mistress and model. The garden features a number of famous statues, including *Le Penseur (The Thinker)*. The charming museum and the beautiful garden can be visited separately.
79 rue de varenne, 7th arr., www.musee-rodin.fr, t: 0144186110, open tue & thu-sun 10am-5:45pm, wed 10am-8:45pm, museum entrance €9, garden €2, metro varenne / invalides

⑳ Since 1920 **Hôtel d'Avaray,** recognizable by the lions above the enormous door, has been the official residence of the Dutch ambassador to France. This house has been the set of numerous French films, including *The Intouchables, Haute Cuisine,* and *Capital.* The gorgeous residence is exclusively for professional use and is therefore not open to the public.
85 rue de grenelle, 7th arr., not open to the public, metro rue du bac

㉒ **Musée d'Orsay** is housed in a 19th-century train station that was converted to a museum in 1986. The enormous train station's clock still hangs in the grand hall. Sculptures line the wide balconies, and in the exhibit halls you'll find a collection of Impressionist paintings. The museum has two great restaurants worth trying in addition to the café. The restaurants are only open to museum visitors.

1 rue de bellechasse, 7th arr., www.musee-orsay.fr, t: 0140494814, open tue-wed & fri-sun 9:30am-6pm, thu 9:30am-9:45pm, entrance €11, metro solférino / assemblée nationale / concorde / tuileries

㉓ **Jeu de Paume** (literally "palm game", an early form of tennis) got its name from the fact that in 1851, Napoleon III played tennis in the hall of the building. For the past few years, this building has housed the Centre National de la Photographie, where you can see modern photography exhibits from big names such as Ed Ruscha, Cindy Sherman, Martin Parr, and Helena Almeida.

1 place de la concorde, 8th arr., www.jeudepaume.org, t: 0147031250, open tue 11am-9pm, wed-sun 11am-7pm, entrance €10, metro concorde

㉕ **Musée de l'Orangerie** was once a greenhouse where oranges were grown. The main attraction here is Claude Monet's famous painting *Les Nymphéas (Water Lilies)*. You can also check out the Walter-Guillaume collection, with works from 20th-century painters.

jardin tuileries, 1st arr., www.musee-orangerie.fr, t: 014504300, open mon & wed-sun 9am-6pm, entrance €9, metro concorde

㉖ **Place de la Concorde,** the biggest square in Paris, was the backdrop of bloody scenes during the French Revolution: The guillotine stood here. It was following this tense time that the square received its current name, which makes reference to harmony. In the middle stands the 3,000-year old Luxor obelisk, gifted to the French king Louis-Philippe in 1831 by the Egyptian viceroy Muhammad Ali.

place de la concorde, 1st arr., metro concorde

㉗ **Le Petit Palais** houses the Musée des Beaux-Arts de la Ville de Paris. There is a large collection of artwork here, including works from artists Ingres,

Delacroix, and Courbet, among others. The café in the courtyard is a secret oasis.

avenue winston churchill, 8th arr., www.petitpalais.paris.fr, t: 0153434000, open tue-sun 10am-6pm, free entrance permanent collection, metro champs-élysées clemenceau / concorde

(29) **Le Grand Palais** was built for the 1900 World's Fair, together with Le Petit Palais and the Pont Alexandre III. It is made of concrete, steel, and glass. The enormous glass ceiling is particularly impressive. Inside the building you'll find, among other things, temporary exhibitions (Galeries Nationales du Grand Palais) and a science museum (Palais de la Découverte).

3 avenue du général eisenhower, 8th arr, www.grandpalais.fr, t: 0144131717, see website for opening hours and prices, metro champs-élysées clémenceau / franklin roosevelt

(37) In 1806, one year after the victory at Austerlitz, Napoleon commissioned the construction of the **Arc de Triomphe.** It wasn't until 1836, however, that the Arc was completed. The four large reliefs on the pillars' pedestal commemorate Napoleon's 1805 victory. From the top, you can look out over the Champs-Élysées. Opening hours are dependent on the weather.

place charles de gaulle, 8th arr., www.arc-de-triomphe.monuments-nationaux.fr, t: 0155377377, open daily april-sept 10am-11pm, oct-march 10am-10:30pm, entrance €9.50, metro charles de gaulle-étoile

FOOD & DRINK

(3) Find a seat on the ground floor of **Monsieur Bleu** or on the terrace and enjoy the gorgeous view out over the Seine and the Eiffel Tower. The interior is modern, elegant, and calm, and the tables are quite spaciously placed for a Parisian restaurant. This is a trendy place, with DJs to create a nice atmosphere for dinner. The Eastern-style tuna steak is highly recommended.

20 avenue de new york, 16th arr., monsieurbleu.com, t: 0147209047, open daily noon-2pm & 8pm-10:30pm, price €35, metro iéna / alma-marceau

⑦ On the rooftop of the Musée du Quai Branly you'll find fine-dining restaurant **Les Ombres,** known for its romantic view of the Eiffel Tower. Expect delicious, refined food in small portions.

27 quai branly, 7th arr., www.lesombres-restaurant.com, t: 0147536800, open daily noon-2:15pm & 7pm-10:30pm, price €40, metro alma marceau / rer pont de l'alma

⑪ **Faust** is located under Pont Alexandre III and offers three options: a terrace for something to drink, an elegant restaurant, and a club. If you keep walking under the bridge you'll find many more terraces. This is a particularly hopping place on Friday nights during the summer months.

pont alexandre III, 7th arr., www.faustparis.fr, t: 0144186060, terrace open daily noon-2am, restaurant tue-sun noon-11pm, club thu-sat 11pm-5am, price set lunch €26, metro champs-élysées clemenceau / invalides / assemblée nationale

⑯ **Coutume Café** is the place to go in this embassy area for a special coffee, lunch or weekend brunch. Coffee aficionados come here to buy exotic beans. On Saturday and Sunday you can choose from three types of brunch: classic, detox veggie, or Sumatran. Whatever you opt for, you're sure to leave with a full belly.

47 rue de babylone 7th arr., www.coutumecafe.com, t: 0145515047, open mon-fri 8:30am-7pm, sat-sun 10am-7pm, brunch sat-sun 11am-4pm, price lunch €17, brunch €23, metro st francois xavier

㉘ One of the best hidden terraces in Paris is **Minipalais.** The high marble columns and white stone will make you feel as if you've been transported to Rome. From certain places you can look right into the Grand Palais. At night the terrace is beautifully lit, which gives it an even more romantic feel.

3 avenue winston churchill, 8th arr., www.minipalais.com, t: 0142564242, open daily 10am-2am, price €28, metro champs-elysees clemenceau

㉛ The concept at **Wine by One** is new and futuristic. At this wine bar you get a debit card of sorts from the register, which you can use to choose your own wine from among the hundred bottles. Have a small sip, a half glass or a full glass. Round things off and order a cheese platter to go with your drink.

27 rue de marignan, 8th arr., www.winebyone.com, t: 0145631898, open mon-sat noon-11pm, price €3-12, metro franklin roosevelt

㉜ In the mood for a cocktail? Take a seat in the courtyard of the **Hôtel Pershing Hall,** where a unique vertical garden hangs on the wall. Even if you're not a guest in the hotel, you can come here for breakfast, lunch or drinks.

49 rue pierre charron, 8th arr., www.pershinghall.com, t: 0158365836, open tue-sat 7am-2am, sun-mon 7am-1am, price €32, metro franklin roosevelt

㉟ **Le Drugstore,** inspired by places in New York, is an ideal spot for a business lunch, and the service is designed to accommodate this. Come here for quick, friendly service and excellent food. Le Drugstore is located in the Publicis building, one of France's best-known businesses. There is also a pharmacy open 24 hours a day, a bookstore, and a small grocery store.

133 avenue des champs-élysées, 8th arr., www.publicisdrugstore.com, t: 0144437764, open mon-fri 8am-2am, sat-sun 10am-2am, price €26, metro charles de gaulle-étoile

㊱ When you have something to celebrate, go to **Le Chiberta.** Guy Savoy's stylish restaurant has a Michelin star. Here you can enjoy classic, refined French cuisine. The wine menu is outstanding—and the bottles are even incorporated into the décor.

3 rue arsène houssaye, 8th arr., www.lechiberta.com, t: 0153534200, open mon-fri noon-2:30pm & 7:30pm-11pm, sat 7pm-11:30pm, price tasting menu €110, metro charles de gaulle-étoile

SHOPPING

⑮ At **Ciné Images** you'll find posters of the most diverse films, from French to international, and modern to old. If you've been looking for years for one particular poster, you'll probably find it here. There is a catalogue on the website, so you can prepare your visit beforehand.

68 rue de babylone, 7th arr., www.cine-images.com, t: 0147056025, open tue-fri 10am-1pm & 2pm-7pm, sat 2pm-7pm, metro st francois xavier

⑰ The luxury department store **Le Bon Marché Rive Gauche** is mostly visited by Parisians. You can find all of the high-end brands here. During the week it's nice to take your time and enjoy looking around. There is a second Le Bon Marché store at number 38 La Grande Épicerie de Paris, which is all about gourmet food—an absolute must-see for foodies.

24 rue de sèvres, 7th arr., www.lebonmarche.com, t: 0144398000, open mon-wed & sat 10am-8pm, thu-fri 10am-9pm, la grande épicerie opens at 8:30am, metro sèvres babylone

(18) The concept for the **Conran Shop,** an enormous store full of design items, gadgets and things for the home, was imported from London. You'll find the perfect mix of design classics and new items by young designers at this popular shop.

117 rue du bac, 7th arr., www.conranshop.fr, t: 0142841001, open mon-fri 10am-7pm, sat 10am-7:30pm, metro sèvres babylone

(19) The amazing baked goods from the exclusive **La Pâtisserie des Rêves** are displayed in glass orbs. This is where you'll get the best *mille-feuille* (traditional puff pastry with a custard filling) in Paris.

93 rue du bac, 7th arr., www.lapatisseriedesreves.com, t: 0142840082, open tue-sat 9am-8pm, sun 9am-6pm, metro rue du bac

(21) **Deyrolle** is an experience in and of itself. Creaking floors, old cases full of rarities, butterflies, and seashells and taxidermy animals everywhere—there's so much to see. Above all, for more than 100 years the shop has been making beautiful educational materials, which you'll find plenty of here.

46 rue du bac, 7th arr., www.deyrolle.com, t: 0142223007, open mon 10am-1pm & 2pm-7pm, tue-sat 10am-7pm, metro rue du bac

(24) The **Librairie des Jardins,** which specializes in all things green, is located just inside the Jardin des Tuileries. Under the vaulted ceiling you'll find some 4,000 books and magazines about gardens, parks, flowers, herbs, and more.

place de la concorde, 1st arr., www.louvre.fr, t: 0142606161, open daily 10am-7pm, metro concorde

(33) **Kusmi Tea** is well-known for its delicious tea blends sold in fun, colorful tins. The brand was founded by Pavel Michailovitch Kousmichoff in St.-Petersburg in

1867, and quickly became famous for supplying the tsar's court. When the founder's son was forced into exile during the October Revolution in 1917, he set up shop in Paris. Above the store is Café Kousmichoff, where you can taste tea—hot or iced, by itself or in one of the many tea cocktails on the menu.

71 avenue des champs-élysées, 8th arr., www.cafekousmichoff.com, t: 0145630808, open mon-fri 8am-6pm, sat-sun 10am-6pm, metro franklin roosevelt / george v

(34) Louis Ernest Ladurée opened **Ladurée** in 1862. Little has changed inside since the chic bakery and tea salon first opened. The choice of delectables here is endless, though you must try their famous macarons. Pierre Desfontaines, a French baker and cousin of the owner, has been credited by some with their creation in the early part of the 20th century. The restaurant is a great spot for breakfast.

75 avenue des champs-élysées, 8th arr., www.laduree.com, t: 0140750875, open mon-fri 7:30am-11pm, sat-sun 8am-11:30pm, price macaron starting at €1.50, metro george v

MORE TO EXPLORE

⑧ You will literally get to see another side of the city by visiting its sewers. **Les Égouts de Paris** is a sort of visitor's center where you can see how the city's sewer system is organized. The tour, an initiative set up by the municipality, takes you on an interesting route, with an explanation available in English. Bring an extra sweater though, because it can be significantly colder underground compared to above.

across from 93 quai d'orsay, 7th arr., t: 0153682781, open sat-wed 11am-5pm, price €4.40, metro alma-marceau / rer pont de l'alma

⑨ The city of Paris recently closed **Les Berges de Seine** to cars and opened it for recreation. Now Parisians can stroll, walk, bike, skate, and jog to their hearts' content along this stretch of the river. In summer especially you'll find many activities here. This is an ideal spot for taking a nice walk along the Seine.

between pont de l'alma and the louvre along the seine, lesberges.paris.fr, free entrance, metro alma-marceau / invalides / assemblée nationale / rer pont de l'alma

⑭ In the authentic 19th-century **La Pagode** you'll find a beautiful Japanese movie theater, which has been declared a historical monument. Watching a movie here is a special experience. The garden is also worth a visit, perhaps for a cup of tea. There are no set hours for the bar, so don't be disappointed if it's not open when you're here.

57 bis rue de babylone, 7th arr., t: 0145554848, entrance €9.80, metro st francois xavier

㉚ The **Champs-Élysées,** *la plus belle avenue du monde* (the most beautiful avenue in the world), is a street where you can shop endlessly in chain stores. The side streets Avenue Montaigne and Avenue George V are home to the flagship stores of brands such as Dior, Chanel, and all other major French fashion names.

champs-élysées, 8th arr., metro charles de gaulle-étoile / george v / champs-élysées clemenceau

WALK **6**

BELLEVILLE, CANAL ST.-MARTIN & MENILMONTANT

ABOUT THE WALK

This walk takes you through working-class neighborhoods and artsy areas. You can stop for lunch along the way, hang out in a park or mingle among the locals for a picnic for the water. The Bassin de la Villette and Canal St.-Martin are especially fun in the afternoon. You can easily do this walk either forward or backward. There are very few famous sights or attractions along the route aside from the Père-Lachaise cemetery, which you can also reach directly by Métro.

THE NEIGHBORHOODS

The working-class neighborhoods of Belleville, Canal St.-Martin, and Ménilmontant are located in the 10th and 19th arrondissements on the Right Bank. In recent years more and more hip spots have been popping up near the Canal St.-Martin and **Bassin de la Villette,** from secondhand shops and hotels to great restaurants and cultural hot spots. Even just relaxing along the water—walking, biking, and picnicking—is a good time.

The landscaping in **Parc des Buttes-Chaumont** is one of a kind. From the highest point of the *buttes* (hills) you can look out over **Sacré-Coeur** and the blue-collar Belleville neighborhood, where Édith Piaf grew up. You can still get a taste of the Paris of yesteryear in this neighborhood.

In the middle of Belleville is a small, little-known park called **Parc de Belleville.** The view from the top is amazing. Walking up the hill here is much better than spending hours in line for the Eiffel Tower—of which you get a good view from here. The small streets near the park are full of unique shops, including some great pop-up stores where young designers sell their products. Note that this area doesn't really come to life until after lunch.

Over the years, the southern part of Belleville has taken on a very multicultural dimension. The main roads are defined by Chinese restaurants, exotic grocery stores, and colorful markets. This is where the Ménilmontant neighborhood begins. The main attraction here is the famous **Père-Lachaise cemetery**. This area has been revamped recently but has not lost any of its original character. Unique stores are interspersed among cafés and bars that are especially popular among the young crowd. **Rue Oberkampf** is a particularly lively spot.

SHORT ON TIME? HERE ARE THE HIGHLIGHTS
+ CANAL ST.-MARTIN + BASSIN DE LA VILLETTE + PARC DES BUTTES-CHAUMONT + PARC DE BELLEVILLE + CIMETIERE DU PERE-LACHAISE

TIPS

// Ideal for experienced visitors
// Best on a weekend afternoon
// Not suitable for biking

SIGHTS & ATTRACTIONS

⑨ The largest, most famous cemetery in Paris is the **Cimetière du Père-Lachaise.** This is the final resting place of many famous people, including Oscar Wilde, Marcel Proust, Sidonie-Gabrielle Colette, Édith Piaf, Jim Morrison, and Frédéric Chopin. As you walk through the shaded, chestnut-lined lanes, you'll see graves of all types: mini palaces, crumbling ruins, graves decorated with marble columns, figures of angels, porcelain statues, and much more.

58 rue des rondeaux, boulevard de ménlilmontant, rue des repos, 20th arr., www.pere-lachaise.com, t: 0155258210, open nov 6-march 15: mon-fri 8am-5:30pm, sat 8:30am-5:30pm, sun 9am-5:30pm, march 16-nov 5: mon-fri 8am-6pm, sat 8:30am-6pm, sun 9am-5:30pm, free entrance, metro père lachaise

⑫ **Ateliers d'Artistes de Belleville** is an organization for local artists. The exhibits often display photography and paintings, and are truly worth a visit.

1 rue francis picabia, 20th arr., www.ateliers-artistes-belleville.fr, t: 0177126313, see website for opening hours, metro couronnes

㉚ Édith Piaf was born on December 15, 1915 at number 72 Rue de Belleville. She grew up on the streets of Belleville and Ménilmontant. At the **Musée Édith Piaf** you can learn all about her turbulent life through souvenirs, photos, letters, posters, theater costumes, and more. If you are planning to visit the museum, be sure to make an appointment at least two days beforehand.

5 rue crespin du gast, 11th arr., t: 0143555272, open mon-wed 1pm-6pm, closed june & sept, visit by appointment, free entrance, metro ménilmontant

FOOD & DRINK

① **La Rotonde** is a great location with something for everyone: a restaurant—which also serves brunch, an enormous terrace, and a small bar with music on the weekends. They regularly organize a variety of activities, such as flea markets or fashion brunches. See the website for the most up-to-date program.

6-8 place de la bataille de stalingrad, 19th arr., www.larotonde.com, t: 0180483340, open tue-sat 9am-midnight, sun noon-8pm, price €18, metro jaurès/stalingrad

③ Borrow some chaises lounges and *pétanque* balls at the alternative **Bar Ourcq,** then order your drinks at the bar and head right over to the water. Thanks to the DJ music and yummy snacks, like pigs in a blanket or homemade cake, it is easy to spend an entire evening hanging out here.

68 quai de la loire, 19th arr., barourcq.free.fr, t: 0142401226, open wed-thu 3pm-midnight, fri-sat 3pm-2am, sun 3pm-10pm, price €3, metro jaurès/laumière

⑤ A drink at **Rosa Bonheur,** a former pavilion, is indeed true *bonheur* (happiness). On summer days, their patio is a great place to sit and enjoy a bottle of house wine and a selection of tapas you choose yourself at the bar inside. From Thursday to Sunday starting at 6:00pm is a *guinguette,* which involves drinks, tapas, and dancing to DJ music. The atmosphere is very laidback, and you sit at long wooden tables conducive to making small talk with those around you.

2 avenue des cascades, 19th arr., www.rosabonheur.fr, t: 0142000045, open wed-sun noon-midnight, price tapas €7, metro botzaris/buttes-chaumont

⑩ When you're in the mood for a drink, there is no better place to go than **Moncoeur Belleville.** From the terrace, the view out over the rooftops of Paris is downright spectacular, and inside is pleasant, too. Come here more for a drink and the atmosphere than for the food, although the offerings are decent. The venue also organizes regular exhibits, readings, debates, and music shows.

1 rue des enverges, 20th arr., moncoeurbelleville.com, t: 0143663854, open mon-wed 10:30am-2am, thu-sun 10am-2am, price €16, sunday brunch €17, metro pyrénées

⑬ **Le Baratin** is a typical Parisian bistro with a perfect wine menu. Raquel Caréla serves up traditional French fare in her small kitchen. Order a glass of Sagesse de Gramenon with lunch or let them suggest something for you. This is a favorite spot among locals, so reservations are recommended.

3 rue jouye-rouve, 20th arr., t: 0143493970, open mon noon-2:30pm, tue-fri noon-2:30pm & 7pm-11pm, sat 7pm-11pm, price lunch €20, dinner €40, metro pyrénées/belleville

⑭ You'll think you're in Colombia at **Múkura,** thanks to the restaurant's colorful décor, the tropical fruit for sale here, and the owner—who hails from Colombia—

who is always here to greet you. The food is prepared Colombian-style. Order delicious cocktails while you wait. Satisfaction guaranteed.

82 rue rebeval, 19th arr., www.mukura.fr, t: 0142493405, open thu-sat noon-4pm & 7pm-11pm, sun noon-11pm, price €23, metro jourdain/pyrénées

⑯ In the mood for a French-Cambodian meal? At **Le Petit Cambodge** you can get lunch or dinner Cambodian-style. Slide up to one of the narrow wooden tables and dig in with chopsticks. You can come here any time of the day.

20 rue alibert, 10th arr., www.lepetitcambodge.fr, t: 0142458088, open daily noon-11pm, price €13, metro république/goncourt

⑲ **La Chambre aux Oiseaux** is the perfect spot for breakfast, tea, coffee, cake, amazing organic drinks, or Sunday brunch. The colorful wallpaper and furniture are reminiscent of grandma's house and make for an inviting atmosphere.

48 rue bichat, 10th arr., lachambreauxoiseaux.tumblr.com, t: 0140189849, open tue-sun 10am-6:30pm, price lunch or tea and cake €10, brunch €20, metro république/goncourt

㉒ Looking for delicious gluten-free French baked goods? You're in the right place at **Helmut Newcake.** Cheesecake, cream puffs or chocolate cake—there's plenty to choose from. Get your pastries to go or take a seat at one of the inviting tables and enjoy them on the spot. The comfy chairs in the back are particularly enticing. At lunchtime you're encouraged to order a meal from the lunch menu.

36 rue bichat, 10th arr., www.helmutnewcake.com, t: 0982590039, open mon-sat noon-7:30pm, sun 10am-6pm, price lunch €9, sunday brunch €24, metro république/goncourt

㉓ Restaurant **Le Chateaubriand** is incredibly popular. And for good reason—the talented young chef Inaki Aizpitarte serves up top-quality, innovative dishes in a beautiful, simple and stylish setting. The wait staff also look sharp, adding that little finishing touch to the restaurant's overall concept. Reservations are an absolute must.

129 avenue parmentier, 11th arr., www.lechateaubriand.net, t: 0143574595, open tue-sat 7:30pm-11pm, price set meal €70, metro goncourt

㉙ **Café Charbon** was originally a variety theater where singer Maurice Chevalier made his debut. The grand café, with its dark wood interior and lights that appear to have been hanging for centuries, is always packed on the weekend with young Parisians. Come here at night for a drink, to catch a live show, and maybe even to dance.

109 rue oberkampf, 11th arr., t: 0143575513, open sun-wed 9am-2am, thu-sat 9am-4am, price €15, metro parmentier

㉛ **Le Perchoir** has a Parisian *Sex and the City* feel. At this rooftop bar you can lounge with a cocktail in hand while looking out at a view of the city. The clientele is international—residents from all parts of the city come here to meet up. Le Perchoir is not immediately visible from the street. Take the elevator where the bouncer is standing, and it will bring you up seven stories to the rooftop bar. There is a selection of French bar food to order from, and the restaurant (reservation required) is one floor down.

14 rue crespin du gast, 11th arr., leperchoir.fr, t: 0148061848, open bar mon-fri 4pm-2am, sat-sun 2pm-2am, restaurant tue-sat 8pm-10:30pm, price drink €13, set meal €48, metro ménilmontant/rue st.-maur

SHOPPING

⑥ Anyone looking for unique designer items must definitely stop in at **L'Embellie.** Ceramics, lamps, office goods and bags are just a few of the items from the store's full collection. You can be sure that whatever products you come across here, you won't find anywhere else. The street is full of pop-up stores that sell local design items. Be sure to stop in and check some of them out.

14 rue de la villette, 19th arr., www.lembellie-design.fr, t: 0142014289, open tue-sat 11am-2pm & 4pm-8pm, very occasionally on sunday 11am-1pm, metro jourdain

⑳ **Antoine & Lili** consists of three brightly colored shops on the Canal St.-Martin. One of the stores sells objects from around the world, one sells women's apparel, and one sells kids' clothes. All three are multicultural havens of clothing and kitsch that come in styles ranging from Hindustani to Mexican. You'll also find all of Antoine and Lili's favorite brands alongside the stores' own clothing line.

95 quai de valmy, 10th arr., www.antoineetlili.com, t: 0140374155, open mon-fri 11am-8pm, sat 10am-8pm, sun 10am-7pm, metro république/goncourt

㉑ Outlet stores for numerous French brands are tucked away in **Rue de Marseille.** You'll find collections from the previous season and discounted items from stores such as Maje (number 4), Claudie Pierlot (number 6) and Les Petites (number 11). Enjoy browsing through the large selection of tiny dresses, shoes, silk blouses, leather jackets, handbags, and more.

rue de marseille, 10th arr., www.sofrenchy.net/stocks-from-rue-de-marseille-the-fashion-shop, open mon-sat 11am-8pm, sun 1:30pm-7:30pm, metro jacques bonsergent/république/goncourt

㉔ At **Africouleur,** you'll find dresses, skirts, shoes, scarves, hats, kids' clothes, and linens made from traditional African material with a modern Western twist. All items are also available on the store's website.

108 rue st.-maur, 11th arr., www.africouleur.com, t: 0156981535, open tue-sat 10:30am-8:30pm, metro rue st-maur/parmentier

㉕ **Au Nouveau Nez** has racks of carefully selected, high-quality wines and champagnes. The selection is small but varied and surprising, and includes organic wines. If you want to immediately taste your purchase you can open your bottle on the spot—then get some tapas to go with it.

112-114 rue st.-maur, 11th arr., t: 0143550230, open tue 4pm-9pm, wed-sat 3pm-10pm, metro rue st.-maur/parmentier

㉖ Looking for a funny gift? **L'Auto école** sells unique items and accessories, such as fur wallets and spunky wire necklaces. You are sure to find something that strikes your fancy among the numerous curious objects here.

101 rue oberkampf, 11th arr., t: 0143553194, open mon 4pm-0:30pm, tue-fri noon-2pm & 2:30pm-8:30pm, sat noon-8:30pm, metro parmentier/rue st.-maur

㉗ The collection of bags, jewelry, and accessories at **Made by Moi** are—as the name suggests—all handmade. Some items are produced in small batches, while

others are one-of-a-kind. You'll also find a small selection of clothes and knick-knacks here.

86 rue oberkampf, 11th arr., www.madebymoi.fr, t: 0158309578, open mon 2:30pm-8pm, tue-sat 10am-8pm, metro parmentier

㉘ You can't walk past **L'Imagigraphe** without noticing its bright orange store-front. The store is innovative when it comes to music and images and is chock full of books, stationary, CDs, and DVDs. Ask at the register for a program if you're interested in attending a reading by a writer or artist.

84 rue oberkampf, 11th arr., www.imagigraphe.fr, t: 0148075420, open mon-wed & fri-sat 10am-8pm, thu 10am-9pm, metro parmentier

MORE TO EXPLORE

② At the end of a good day, **Bassin de la Villette** is a nice place to walk along the water, stop, sit awhile, have a picnic or play a game of *pétanque*. Groups of friends gather here for picnics and drinks. On both sides of the water there are theaters where you can catch a movie. Buy a ticket on the opposite side of the water from where your film is showing, and cross to the other side by boat.

quai de la loire, metro jaurès/stalingrad

④ Buttes-Chaumont was once a place of marshy land and chalky soil. In 1864, Napoleon III commissioned the urban architect Haussmann to take control of this no-man's land and, in 1867, the **Parc des Buttes-Chaumont** was opened. The park is a wonderful landscape of trees, shrubs, stairs, caves, and a big lake. The lake contains a large rock with a replica of Tivoli's Temple de Sybille on top. Go up the paths and stairs to the temple and you'll be rewarded with a surprising view of the Sacré-Coeur.

rue manin, rue botzaris, avenue simon-bolivar, 19th arr., butteschaumont.free.fr, open daily: may-sept 7am-10pm, oct-april 7am-8pm, free entrance, metro buttes-chaumont/botzaris

⑦ Near the beautiful street Villa de l'Ermitage is the **Studio de l'Ermitage:** A concert hall, cinema, and theater. Visit their website and see what the program lists—it's definitely worth it. Villa l'Ermitage is like a bit of countryside in the middle of Paris. It's nice to walk around, take photos of the colorfully shuttered houses and admire the artistic graffiti. Who knows, you might even see an artist busy at work.

8 rue de l'ermitage, 20th arr., www.studio-ermitage.com, t: 0144620286, open daily 8:30pm-2am, entrance €8-15, metro ménilmontant/jourdain/gambetta

⑧ The Sunday jazz brunch at **La Bellevilloise** always draws a crowd. Enjoy a buffet of sweet and savory French fare under the olive trees in the Halle aux Oliviers, and be sure to check out the program beforehand so you're up to date on what's going on in this culture center. Exhibits, dance performances, concerts, clubs—anything is possible. The clientele at La Bellevilloise is hip and alternative. Next door, La Maroquinerie (at 23 Rue Boyer) is a similar venue, with cultural events and a restaurant where you can spend an enjoyable evening.

19-21 rue boyer, 19th arr., www.labellevilloise.com, t: 0146360707, open wed-thu 7pm-1am, fri 7pm-2am, sat 11am-2am or 6pm-2am (depends on program), sun 11:30am-5pm (brunch 11:30am & 2pm), entrance €10-20, jazz brunch €29, metro ménilmontant/jourdain/gambetta

⑪ Built in 1988 against a steep hill, **Parc de Belleville** is the highest park in Paris. Although small, the park is not to be missed. Go for the phenomenal view of the city if nothing else. Walk down the beautiful paths—up and down stairs, past springs that once supplied the city's water and along waterfalls that feed into lakes below.

rue piat, rue des couronnes, rue julien-lacroix, 20th arr., open winter: mon-fri 8am-7pm, sat-sun 9am-7pm, summer mon-fri 8am-9:30pm, sat-sun 9am-7:30pm, free entrance, metro pyrénées/couronnes

⑮ **Place Sainte-Marthe** is one of Paris's best-hidden gems. Savor the calm in one of two bistros. There are often musicians on the square and sometimes small theater performances.

place ste.-marthe, 10th arr., metro colonel fabien/belleville

⑰ Built between 1821 and 1825, **Le Canal St.-Martin** is about four kilometers (2.5 miles) long. A system of locks regulates the water levels, which differ from

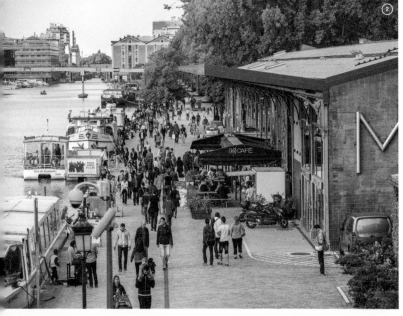

one end of the canal to the other by over 25 meters (82 feet). The beautiful cast-iron bridges often appear in movies. In *Amélie,* the main character is seen skipping stones over the water here. The up-and-coming neighborhood around the canal is full of nice cafés and unique clothing stores.

le canal st.-martin, 10th arr., metro république/goncourt

⑱ **Le Comptoir Général** is an alternative hub of the kind you might come across in Berlin or Barcelona, but not often in Paris. This culture center was built in an old stable and is decorated in French-African colonial style. The shabby chic decor gives it a mysterious atmosphere. There are lots of hidden nooks where you might come across a curio cabinet or a glass case filled with exotic plants. Order a fresh ginger juice at the bar or eat fried banana in the restaurant, which is really more of an often-full dining hall. This is a great spot for an aperitif, brunch, cultural reading or film.

80 quai de jemmapes, 10th arr., www.lecomptoirgeneral.com, t: 0144882045, open daily 11am-1am, price voluntary donation, metro république/goncourt

㉜ **Le Gossima** is Paris's first ping-pong bar, where you can not only get something to drink but can also play table tennis. Come with friends to this spacious bar full of ping-pong tables for a night of fun and games—it's a nice alternative to a pool hall. On Friday evenings, the venue occasionally organizes ping-pong disco night. The crowd here is primarily twenty- and thirty-somethings. Le Gossima has been a popular hotspot since it opened in 2014.

4 rue victor gelez, 11th arr., www.gossima.fr, t: 0967297579, open mon 4pm-midnight, tue-sat 4pm-2am, free entrance, ping-pong table rental €6, metro ménilmontant/rue st.-maur

WITH MORE TIME

The walks in this book will take you to most of the city's main highlights. Of course, there are still a number of places worth visiting and things worth seeing that are not included in these walks. You'll find them listed them below. Note that not all of these places are easily accessible by foot from the center of town, but you can get to them all using public transportation.

Ⓐ In 2014, the 18th arrondissement decided to spruce up a dilapidated Métro station along the line known as *la petite ceinture* in the northern part of the city. Now you can head to **La Recyclerie** for brunch (on Saturdays and Sundays), lunch, dinner, or a drink. This is a delightful place to sit on a warm summer's night out in the fresh air at one of the long tables amidst the colorful lights. Events such as flea markets and workshops are regularly held here. La Recyclerie is perfect to combine with a trip to the nearby flea market Marché aux Puces de St.-Ouen.

83 boulevard ornano, 18th arr, www.larecyclerie.com, t: 0142575849, open daily noon-10pm, check website for additional information, price lunch €10, brunch €22, metro porte de clignancourt

Ⓑ At the *marchés aux puces* (flea markets) you can come across some good finds, but don't count on them always being cheap. **Marché aux Puces de St.-Ouen** is Paris's largest antique and flea market—an entire village of antique shops. The flea market is often used as a backdrop in movies, such as *Midnight in Paris*. There are a number of nice cafés here, such as Chez Louisette (136 Avenue Michelet), where you can get lunch and listen to real French *chansons* sung live.

avenue de la porte de clignancourt, 18th arr., www.marcheauxpuces-saintouen. com, open sat-mon 10am-6pm, metro porte de clignancourt

Ⓒ In the middle of the Bois de Boulogne you'll find the **Fondation Louis Vuitton** museum, which opened in 2015. The futuristic building alone, designed by Frank Gehry, makes it worth a visit. Inside, you'll find a permanent collection as well as temporary exhibits of modern and contemporary art. Occasionally there are classical concerts. Come to the restaurant Le Frank for an outstanding

lunch and, on Wednesday and Thursday evenings, for a themed dinner
(reservations required).

8 avenue du mahatma gandhi, 16th arr, www.fondationlouisvuitton.fr, t: 0140699600,
open mon & wed-thu noon-7pm, fri noon-11pm, sat-sun 11am-8pm, entrance €14,
metro les sablons (15-minute walk) or shuttle bus from place charles de gaulle
(corner of avenue de friedland)

Ⓓ **La Cinémathèque Française** is located in the former Centre Culturel
Américain, a building designed by architect Frank Gehry. The archive contains
some 14,000 films and an enormous collection of documents, manuscripts,
posters, and even costumes worn by Hollywood legends such as Greta Garbo
and Elizabeth Taylor. In addition to the permanent exhibit about the history of
film, there are also exhibits with unique film screenings and readings.

51 rue de bercy, 12th arr., www.cinematheque.fr, t: 0171193333, open mon & wed-
sat noon-7pm, sun 10am-8pm, entrance museum €5, exhibition €11, film €6.50,
metro bercy

(E) Train tracks ran across **Le Viaduc des Arts** from 1859 to 1969. In 1996 it was transformed into a *promenade plantée:* a 4.5km-long park (2.8 miles). Take the stairs at the beginning of the street and walk over the 64 red brick arches. In the archways you'll find workshops and stores.

avenue daumesnil, 12th arr., www.leviaducdesarts.fr, t: 0144758066, open daily 10am-7pm, free entrance permanent collection, metro bastille

(F) **Parc de la Villette** has a focus on science and art. The futuristic municipal park has been around since 1986 and includes a playground, a concert hall, an IMAX movie theater *(La Géode)* and a variety of museums. Visit, for example, the Cité des Sciences et de l'Industrie (science museum) and the Cité de la Musique/Philharmonie de Paris (music museum). The park is full of activities, such as free movies in the open-air movie theater in July and August. Check out the website for the latest program. You can easily spend the entire day in Parc de la Villette.

211 avenue jean jaurès, 19th arr., www.villette.com, t: 0140037575, open daily, free entrance to park, museums €7-€16, metro porte de pantin / porte de la villette

(G) **La Tour Montparnasse** is a typical 20th-century monument—209 meters (686 feet) tall, with the fastest elevator in Europe, bringing you to the top in just 38 seconds. The 56th floor features a fantastic panoramic view of Paris, and when the weather is clear, even of the entire Île de France. You can see as far as 40 kilometers (25 miles) away. Daring visitors can visit the open terrace two stories above.

33 avenue du maine, 15th arr., www.tourmontparnasse56.com, t: 0145385256, open daily: april-sept 9:30am-11:30pm, oct-march sun-thu 9:30am-10:30pm, fri-sat 9:30am-11pm, entrance €15, metro montparnasse-bienvenüe

(H) Face the lines and journey into Paris's underworld. Descend 91 steps below ground into the world of the dead and see bones from old burial grounds. There are countless myths about the **Catacombs.** It is cold here, so bring an extra layer.

1 avenue du colonel henri rol-tanguy, 14th arr., www.catacombes.paris.fr, t: 0144595831, open tue-sun 10am-8pm, entrance €10, metro denfert-rochereau

(I) The **Musée Jacquemart-André** was originally the private residence of enthusiastic art collectors. There is a very diverse art collection on display from the 18th century and from the Italian Renaissance. The luxurious tea room is a nice spot for Sunday brunch.

158 boulevard haussmann, 8th arr., www.musee-jacquemart-andre.com, t: 0145621159, open mon 10am-8:30pm, tue-sun 10am-6pm, entrance €12, metro st-philippe du roule / miromesnil / st augustin

(J) The **Marché Aligre** is a lively vegetable market that makes for a nice, busy street scene on Saturday and Sunday mornings. The local residents meet up here to chat about the past week over wine at Le Baron Rouge (1 Rue Théophile Roussel), one of the many cafés at the market.

place d'aligre, 12th arr., open sat-sun 8am-1pm, metro ledru-rollin

(K) **Musée Marmottan Monet** is particularly known for its collection of works by Impressionist painter Claude Monet. You'll also find artworks from the Renaissance and the First Empire in this beautiful 19th-century building. When you're on this side of Paris, reserve a table at the restaurant La Gare (19 Chaussée de la Muette). You can enjoy a delicious meal in the unique environment of this former train station.

2 rue louis boilly, 16th arr., www.marmottan.fr, t: 0144965033, open tue-wed & sat-sun 10am-6pm, thu 10am-9pm, entrance €10, metro la muette

(L) At the corner of Métro station Passy is a sort of underground *cave* (wine cellar): **Musée du Vin.** Visit the interesting and beautiful exhibit about how wine is made, the techniques used in the past and the present, and all the various objects involved in wine making. It is not big—you'll have seen it all in less than an hour. If you know you'll have more time than that, make reservations before-hand for a wine tasting or enjoy lunch in the restaurant. A nice wine is paired with every course.

5 square charles dickens, 16th arr., www.museeduvinparis.com, t: 0145256326, museum open tue-sat 10am-6pm, restaurant tue-sat noon-3pm, museum entrance €10, metro passy

ⓜ Within a half hour of Paris you can be in the pleasant town of Versailles, known for the enormous **Château de Versailles.** This 1631 castle has a rich history. France was ruled from here from 1681 to 1789. The imposing palace, with its enormous gardens, halls, outbuildings, and status symbols, leaves a special impression. You could easily spend several days here. There are firework shows at night in the summer. Tip: Buy your ticket online beforehand.

place d'armes, versailles, www.chateauversailles.fr, t: 0130837800, castle open april-oct tue-sun 9am-6:30pm, park daily 7am-8:30pm, nov-march tue-sun 9am-5:30pm, park daily 8am-6pm, free entrance to park, castle €15 (free first sunday of month), rer c from st.-michel or champ de mars to versailles rive gauche/transilien from st.-lasatre to versailles chantiers

AFTER DARK

When it comes to going out, Paris has something for everyone. Parisians love long, extended dinners in any of the city's thousands of restaurants. Each

neighborhood has its own places to go for a good night. Parisians also enjoy a good movie or show, and there's plenty of selection when it comes to theaters and venues. Pick up a *Pariscope* magazine at any of the many newspaper kiosks around the city to find out what's going on when you're in town.

There's also a lot of choice when it comes to bars and clubs. For the younger student crowd, head to Rue Princesse and Rue des Canettes in the 6th arrondissement. In the mood for a big international dance club? Then go to Grands Boulevards or Place Pigalle. Is a mellow jazz joint or sophisticated nightclub more your style? Find all the latest information about nightlife in Paris on **www.timetomomo.com**—from swanky cocktail and wine bars to popular pubs and clubs. Check it out and plan your own perfect night in Paris.

HOTELS

A good bed, a tasty breakfast, and a nice interior—these are all ingredients for a pleasant hotel stay. Even more important, however, might be location. A hotel is only good if you can walk out of the lobby and straight into the bustling city.

Spending the night in Paris can be pretty pricey, but there are some affordable options. For example, two good options are the charming Hôtel Eldorado between Montmartre and Batignolles and Hôtel Amour, which is located in a residential area in the relatively central 9th arrondissement. Would you rather stay right in the heart of the city so you can access many of the main attractions by foot? Then choose somewhere in the 2nd, 3rd, 4th or 5th arrondissements. In the 7th you can sleep under the Eiffel Tower. And while you might not be right in the thick of things in the 14th, 15th, 19th, and 20th arrondissements, you can find some nice hotels here, such as Mama Shelter. You can find more tips for good hotels on **www.timetomomo.com.**

WWW.TIMETOMOMO.COM

OUR PERSONAL SELECTION OF HOTELS IN THE HOTTEST NEIGHBORHOODS IN TOWN. GO ONLINE & CLICK TO BOOK.

INDEX

✳ INDEX

MOON PARIS WALKS

FIRST EDITION

Avalon Travel
An imprint of Perseus Books
A Hachette Book Group company
1700 Fourth Street
Berkeley, CA 94710, USA
www.moon.com

ISBN 978-1-63121-602-2

Concept & Original Publication "time to momo Parijs" © 2017 by mo'media.
All rights reserved.
For the latest on time to momo walks and recommendations, visit www.timetomomo.com.

MO'MEDIA

TEXT & WALKS
Irene Klein

TRANSLATION
Eileen Holland

MAPS
Van Oort redactie & kartografie

PHOTOGRAPHY
Vincent van den Hoogen, Marion Hoogervorst,
Duncan de Fey

DESIGN
Studio 100% & Oranje Vormgevers

PROJECT EDITORS
Heleen Ferdinandusse, Bambi Bogert

AVALON TRAVEL

PROJECT EDITOR
Sierra Machado

COPY EDITOR
Maggie Ryan

PROOFREADER
Megan Mulholland

COVER DESIGN
Derek Thornton, Faceout Studios

Printed in China by RR Donnelley
First U.S. printing, September 2017.

time to momo

PARIS

100% good time

And to find out more about the latest hot spots, best hotels, nicest neighborhoods, and where to have the most fun in Paris, go to www.timetomomo.com/paris

Individual walks

app